THE ROAD TO APPOMATTOX

BELL IRVIN WILEY

The Road To
Appomattox

LOUISIANA STATE UNIVERSITY PRESS
Baton Rouge and London

To

GEORGE BELL WILEY
whose great-grandfather wore the gray and whose
favorite American is Abraham Lincoln

CONTENTS

ILLUSTRATIONS

Following page 42

Jefferson Davis, the Reluctant Helmsman

The inauguration at Montgomery

Leaders who opposed Davis
Robert Toombs
General Joseph E. Johnston
Robert Barnwell Rhett
Robert Barnwell Rhett, Jr.
William Porcher Miles
Louis T. Wigfall
George W. Randolph

Graph of Confederate Morale 1861-'65

General Lee after Appomattox

General Grant at Spottsylvania

Johnson's *Elementary Arithmetic* 1864

Surrender at Appomattox

The McLean House

Broadside offering reward for Davis' capture

PREFACE

In 1861 eleven Southern states avowed withdrawal from the American Union and set up their own government. When Federal authorities refused to acquiesce in the separation an armed conflict ensued which proved to be in many respects the greatest war that the world had ever known.

At times it seemed that the South's valiant and stubborn effort to achieve independence would succeed. That it did not was due to a combination of causes.

In this little book, the contents of which were presented as the J. P. Young Lectures in American History at Memphis State College in October, 1954, I have dealt with some of the major factors and trends in the Confederacy's decline and defeat. The focus is on the South rather than on the conflict as a whole and principal emphasis is given to high political leadership, morale and internal relationships. The analysis is in part exploratory and some of the conclusions are tentative.

I am indebted to many people and institutions for generously making valuable sources available to me. I am especially grateful to Professor Edward Younger of the University of Virginia for permitting me to read and quote from the diary of Robert G. H. Kean, Chief of the Bureau of War of the Confederate War Department, an exceptionally valuable source that is scheduled for early publication by the Oxford University Press. For financial assistance that enabled me to devote a year to itinerant research I am profoundly grateful to the Henry E. Huntington Library, Emory University and a foundation that modestly chooses to remain anonymous.

BELL IRVIN WILEY
Emory University
5 January 1955

THE ROAD TO APPOMATTOX

Chapter 1   RELUCTANT HELMSMAN:
JEFFERSON DAVIS

ON JANUARY 21, 1861, a tall man who gave the impression of stateliness rose from his seat in the United States Senate to deliver his valedictory. Standing erect despite the illness that plagued him, he calmly surveyed the hushed audience of colleagues and visitors, and then began to speak. His voice, indistinct and faltering at first, soon swelled to its accustomed strength and clarity, and in the words of his wife who sat among the listeners "rang out melodiously clear like a silver trumpet, to the extremest verge of the assembly."

The speaker was Jefferson Davis of Mississippi, experienced, able, respected by the group that he was about to leave. His primary concern since he first entered the Senate in December, 1847, had been the defense of his state and others of the slaveholding community against what he regarded as a growing threat to their sovereign rights under the Federal Constitution. What he said now was in line with the stand that he had taken all along, though he did not re-state all the arguments. He simply asserted, in effect, that Mississippi, despairing of main-

1

taining the rights pledged to the states when the Union was originally formed, had exercised her unquestionable prerogative of secession. In so doing she had surrendered all the benefits of the Union, which were many, but having voluntarily divested herself of these benefits, she claimed "to be exempt from any power to execute the laws of the United States within her limits."

Though always an earnest proponent of slavery and an ardent champion of states' rights, Davis had never been classed as an extremist or a fire-eater, such as Rhett or Yancey. And in some respects he seemed more moderate in 1860 than in 1850. He had a genuine attachment to the Union based on the Revolutionary record of his family and nurtured by his education, army experience, public service and travels. While his belief in the right of secession was unwavering, he appears to have experienced no happiness when the time came for the exercise of that right. His mood when delivering the valedictory was not one of gloating or defiance, but rather one of charity blended with melancholy. "I am sure I feel no hostility to you, Senators from the North," he said. "I hope . . . for peaceful relations with you, though we must part. They may be mutually beneficial to us in the future as they have in the past."

As he concluded his speech his tone became even gentler. "I see now around me some with whom I have served long," he stated; "there have been points of collision; but whatever of offense there has been to me, I leave here; I carry with me no hostile remembrances. . . . I have, Senators, in this our hour of parting to offer you my apology for any pain which, in heat of discussion, I have inflicted. It only remains for me to bid you adieu."

Thus did Jefferson Davis sever his personal and official ties with the Union. He was not a demonstrative person, nor the sort who liked to play on the emotions of others. It is highly significant of the man and the meaning to him of the occasion that as he here said farewell to his colleagues he displayed more feeling than in any other public address of his career. When in the course of his remarks the profound silence was broken by applause his countenance registered rebuke, as he deemed such an exhibition to be out of harmony with the solemnity of the hour. And when he took his seat, "there was scarcely a dry eye" in the audience, according to Mrs. Davis. He was "inexpressibly sad" when he left the Senate chamber, she added, and that night she heard him pray that peaceful councils might prevail.

The valedictory was as brief as it was solemn, requiring probably no more than fifteen minutes in the delivery. But it was one of the most eloquent speeches of Davis's career. Its sentiments would seem unlikely to have marked him at the time the future head of the move for Southern independence. But the circumstances and the time were such that the speech helped make Davis president of the Southern Confederacy.

The choice of Davis to head the new government is one of the great ironies of Southern history. He had not been a central figure in the creation of the Confederacy. He was not a delegate to the Montgomery Convention. He stated emphatically and repeatedly during the war and afterward that he did not want the position of president and there is no reasonable basis for doubting the sincerity of his claim. In his *Rise and Fall of the Confederate Government* published in 1881, Davis professes to have known before the Provisional Congress met at Montgomery that he was among those being considered for the presidency; he also asserts that he took what appeared to be "adequate precautions" to prevent his election. Alexander M. Clayton, one of the Provisional Congressmen from Mississippi, stated not long after the war that he wrote Davis before going to Montgomery asking him if he would accept the Confederate presidency. Davis replied, according to Clayton, "that it was not the place he desired; that if he could have his choice he would greatly prefer to be in active service as commander-in-chief of the army, but that he would give himself to the cause in any capacity whatever."

The sessions of the Provisional Congress were secret. Because of this and the determination to make a show of unanimity in selecting the executive, it is difficult for the historian to reconstruct the events and influences that led to Davis's election. E. A. Pollard, the Richmond editor who made a career of denouncing the Davis administration, claimed that Davis had been agreed on by the Southern congressional delegations in Washington before they left the capital, but no support can be found for this statement. The assertion made by Alexander Stephens after the war that certain delegations at Montgomery backed Davis to head off Howell Cobb, whom they mistakenly thought to be the candidate of the Georgia group, does not jibe with statements made by T. R. R. Cobb in letters written to his wife while the Congress was in session.

There can be no doubt that Davis's reputation for conservatism—the fact of his being identified with no extreme group—commended him to the Provisional Congress. For the delegates sent to Montgomery to organize the Confederate government were for the most part a cautious, sober group, who hoped for peaceful separation from the Union and the quick establishment of a stable and orderly government—and hence desired to keep the fire-eating element in the background. Had this group known how strongly Davis believed in the inevitability of war, they might have been less favorably inclined toward him.

Be that as it may, Davis was chosen, first on a provisional basis by the Congress and later for a full term of six years by a popular election in which he had no opponent. In the brief interval between his withdrawal from the United States Senate and his election as Confederate president, Davis was in Mississippi developing the state's military organization with a commission of major general given to him by Governor J. J. Pettus. When the messenger bearing news of the election found him, Davis was in the garden of his Brierfield plantation helping with rose cuttings. On reading the telegram, "he looked so grieved," according to Mrs. Davis, "that I feared some evil had befallen our family." "After a few minutes painful silence," she continued, "he told me [of the contents] as a man might speak of a sentence of death." But, accepting the action of the Congress as a mandate, he quickly adjusted his plantation affairs and departed the next day for Montgomery. Thus reluctantly did he who longed to lead the Confederacy's armies, assume the direction of its political fortunes.

Davis's election met with enthusiastic response throughout the South. One of those who sent congratulatory messages was David L. Yulee of Florida who wrote the new President on February 13, 1861: "How much I have been delighted by the unanimity with which you have been called to the head of the Southern movement, I need not say. That unanimity was not in the convention alone but in the general hearts of the people. . . . I doubt if Washington in his day had more entire hold upon the public confidence." About the same time a South Carolinian wrote exuberantly to a friend: "All hail to our first Southern President." The Montgomery *Weekly Advertiser* characterized Davis's trip from Jackson, Mississippi, to the Alabama capital as "one continuous ovation," and proudly proclaimed the President as being "in every way equal to the extraordinary crisis of affairs."

On his arrival in Montgomery, Davis received a tremendous welcome, during the course of which William L. Yancey, in one of the most fervid speeches of his career, paid Davis the now classic tribute: "How fortunate is our country. . . . She has found in the distinguished gentleman she has called to preside over her public affairs the statesman, the soldier, the patriot. . . . The man and the hour have met."

After the inauguration ceremonies, Montgomery women wreathed Davis with flowers and according to a local reporter, "ten thousand hearts beat high with joy, admiration and hope for the new president." "No man, not even George Washington," in the words of this admiring journalist, "was ever called on to preside over a people with more general acclamation and confidence than Gen. Davis."

On April 3, 1861, Louis T. Wigfall, who as a Confederate Senator later was to become one of Davis's bitterest opponents, told an enthusiastic audience: "You have shown wisdom in the selection of our President—a man I know well and love truly. . . . He combines all the great, striking and remarkable qualities of your own Calhoun, and of the scarcely less distinguished though not less loved Andrew Jackson. . . . Jefferson Davis has the wisdom and sagacity of the statesman . . . the courage and discretion of the soldier. . . . I know of no man so competent to inaugurate a Government at such a time as Jefferson Davis."

The trip of Davis from Montgomery to the new seat of government in Richmond in May, 1861, called forth other and greater manifestations of enthusiasm. At Atlanta, Augusta, Wilmington and Goldsboro, large crowds acclaimed the President. At Goldsboro, where Davis dined in a local hotel, beautiful girls thronged about him, some "bedecking him with garlands of flowers while others fanned him," as members of a military unit fired guns and a band played inspiriting martial airs—all of which must have gone hard with the ailing guest's chronic dyspepsia.

* * * * *

The recipient of these fulsome tributes possessed many admirable qualities. His family knew him as a kindly, understanding and affectionate husband and father, who in the relaxation of home could charm them with interesting talk, expert mimicry and thrilling stories of frontier experience. Those who knew him only casually thought him humorless. It is true that public manifestations of his humor were rare, especially during the war years, but he was by no means utterly devoid of it. Even as a small boy he displayed a mischievous streak. On returning to Mississippi from a Kentucky school when he was nine he planned to surprise his mother, who had not seen her son for two years. Walking up to the house and finding her sitting near the door he asked her if she had seen any stray horses about the premises. Whereupon, according to Davis's report of the incident in his old age, "She said she had seen a stray boy and clasped me in her arms." Davis occasionally revealed a bantering, fun-loving trait to his associates at Transylvania, West Point and on army posts. In her memoir Mrs. Davis tells of one manifestation of the president's humor during the war. According to her account, Davis one morning received the following letter from a girl whose sweetheart had long been absent in the army:

> 'Dear Mr. President:
>
> I want you to let Jeems C., of company oneth, 5th South Carolina Regiment, come home and get married. Jeems is willin', I is willin', his mammy says she is willin', but Jeems's capt'in, he ain't willin'. Now when we are all willin' 'ceptin' Jeems' captain, I think you might let up and let Jeems come. I'll make him go straight back when he's done got married and fight just as hard as ever.
>
> Your affectionate friend, etc.'

The President wrote on the letter, "Let Jeems go," and in the words of Mrs. Davis, "Jeems went home, married the affectionate correspondent of Mr. Davis, returned to his regiment, and did fight as well as ever."

No one can read Davis's war-time correspondence without being impressed by the warmth and tenderness of his relations with his family. On December 15, 1862, while on a visit to Bragg's army the President wrote his wife: "Kiss my dear children for their loving Father. They can little realize how much I miss them. Every sound is the voice of my child. . . . none can equal their charms, nor can compare with my own long worshipped Winnie—

'She is na my ain Lassie
Though fair the lassie be.
For well ken I my ain Lassie
By the kind love in her eye.'

This letter reveals a touch of poetry in the leader of the Lost Cause.

Davis seems to have shared his thoughts and problems fully with his wife who, despite a tendency of some of the Richmond ladies to disparage her as a crude Westerner, was in every sense a remarkable woman—intelligent, well informed and witty. She was not beautiful, but she was full of sparkle and charm and she and her husband were devoted to each other. The tragic loss of their son who was killed by a fall from a second floor porch in 1864 and the reverses brought by the war drew them very close together. The letters that they exchanged during the anxious period before his capture in 1865, when she addressed him as "my own dear Banny," are full of tenderness and understanding.

Davis was blessed with an impressive appearance and demeanor. He looked and acted like somebody. This is not to say that he was a model of handsomeness, for his hollow cheeks, furrowed face and sharp features gave him a rough-hewn aspect. But his piercing glance, his erect bearing, his calm but decisive address and his dignified, self-assured manner set him apart in a crowd and commanded attention when he spoke. The power of his presence and address was demonstrated when he mounted a carriage during the famous Richmond "bread riot" of April 2, 1863, and dispersed the hoodlums and the hungry who were threatening the peace of the city.

One of the most vivid descriptions of Davis was that of Lieutenant Benjamin Blackford who on August 11, 1862, wrote his homefolk: "Sunday before last I sat in St. Paul's Church near the President. . . . He bears the marks of greatness about him beyond all persons I have ever seen—A perfect head, a deep set eagle eye, an aquiline nose, and mouth and jaw sawed in *steel*—but above all, the *gentleman* is apparent, the *thorough, high-bred,* polished gentleman."

Whatever else may be said of him, Davis, throughout his career as President, in public and in private, in victory and in defeat, conducted himself with a dignity befitting his position.

Another of Davis's advantages was a good education. His early training included two years in a Catholic school in Kentucky and his collegiate career consisted of three years at Transylvania University followed by four years at West Point. His performance in none of these institutions was brilliant (he was graduated twenty-third in a class of thirty-four at West Point), and his real education did not come until after he had completed his formal schooling. In the period 1836-1843, following the death of his first wife, Davis lived in comparative seclusion on a plantation adjoining that of his brother Joe near Vicksburg, Mississippi. For pastime and self-improvement he read extensively during these years of solitude, from the *Congressional Globe* and from works of the founding fathers and other excellent volumes loaned to him by his brother. The reading was supplemented by discussions with Joe, who eventually was rated a millionaire, and who apparently had in mind a political career for his promising young brother and ward. It was through a "Great Books Course," then, provided by brother Joe, that Jefferson Davis became the well-educated person revealed by his subsequent writing and speeches.

Davis's good education was matched by sound character. Some of his bitterest enemies conceded his basic honesty and none to my knowledge charged him with immorality. Alexander Stephens once hinted to Herschel V. Johnson that he suspected Davis of misappropriating secret service funds, and on June 3, 1864, the Vice-President wrote to his brother Linton: "He [Davis] is quite as much knave as fool." But these comments may be dismissed as the ravings of a little man, sick in both mind and body. As president, Davis was not always as forthright as he might have been in dealing with difficult persons and situations but these failings were more than offset by consistent observance of a strict code of conduct with reference to money, favors, gifts and anything else which might bring him or his family into disrepute. "Honest Jeff" would have been no less an appropriate title than was "Honest Abe."

Courage was another of Davis's virtues. His physical bravery was convincingly attested in the Mexican War, and he proved his moral courage repeatedly during the Confederate War by long and firm adherence to unpopular measures and persons.

Another of Davis's assets was fluency. He wrote with commendable clarity and in public address he was unusually effective. His speeches have not the music and the poetry of Lincoln's classic pieces, but they are lucid, logical and stately compositions. Davis's prowess as a speaker was attributable in large part to excellence of delivery. An earnest manner, a dignified bearing, a voice that was soft but clear and a forcefulness of personality that compelled attention—all these combined to give Davis high standing among the public speakers of his time. He was not the soaring type of orator, such as Clay or Webster. Nor was he a master of anecdote and wit. His strength lay in the substance and logic of his remarks and the pleasing, persuasive and even elegant mode of their presentation. If Davis had been as strong in all other respects as he was in public address, the government of the Confederacy might have fared much better than it did.

Davis brought to the presidency extensive experience in public affairs. Entering the National House of Representatives in December, 1845, he served in that body until the summer of 1846, when he resigned to participate in the Mexican War. After his return from Mexico as a wounded hero he entered the United States Senate in December, 1847, where he remained until called back to Mississippi to enter the gubernatorial contest against Henry S. Foote in the autumn of 1851. After defeat by a narrow margin in this race he remained out of public life until March 7, 1853, when he entered Pierce's cabinet as Secretary of War. In 1857 he returned to the United States Senate where he remained until January, 1861. In all these positions Davis acquitted himself with distinction, and the prestige and experience thus gained naturally were considered as facts in his favor when the Confederate fathers at Montgomery were confronted with the necessity of choosing a president.

These fathers also regarded Davis's military experience as a point to his credit; for while peace was the hope of most, war was regarded as a definite possibility. Davis's army duty and his associations while Secretary of War and Chairman of the Senate Committee on Military Affairs gave him an understanding of military terminology, organization and problems that stood him in good stead as Confederate commander-in-chief. Even more important was the knowledge that this experience gave him of military personnel. In sum, Davis knew who was who among the professional soldiery, and he was able to talk understandingly with them about military matters. Even though this knowledge was not always used to the Confederacy's benefit, the possession of it gave Davis a tremendous initial advantage over his opposite in Washington.

A final asset of Davis was a profound and unwavering devotion to the cause that he led. His belief in state sovereignty and the Southern way of life amounted to a deep conviction. He apparently had no qualms about the rightness of slavery, though near the end of the war he indicated a willingness to accept emancipation as a price of Southern independence. Davis's belief in the justice of the Confederate cause seemed to become more intense as the war progressed, and his attachment to it became so strong that it blinded him to the reality of impending defeat. At the time of his capture, after the surrender of Lee's and Johnston's armies, he was making plans for continuance of the struggle in the country beyond the Mississippi. The Confederacy may well have entrusted its destinies to abler men than Davis, but it could not have committed them to one who believed more passionately in the Southern cause or who defended that cause more earnestly.

* * * * *

Such were the qualifications that justified the choice of Davis for the presidency. But if a balance be struck on him, based primarily on his record as president, items on the debit side of the ledger far outweigh those to his credit.

In the first place he was a poor administrator. This deficiency can be attributed in part to lack of executive experience. True, in the pre-presidential period, he had commanded a regiment in the Mexican War, run a plantation in Mississippi, served many years in the national legislature and been Secretary of War. He had been successful in all these activities. But none of them was of such scope as to require outstanding administrative ability or to afford training in large-scale executive techniques. During Davis's years as Secretary of War the effective strength of the regular army was only 15,000, and War Department business in Washington was conducted by a staff of 132 officers and civilians. Even so, Davis's administrative experience compared favorably with that of most public servants of the period. His shortcomings as chief executive of the Confederacy must be charged less to lack of experience than to personality and temperament.

Two prime essentials of effective administration are able assistants and delegation of authority. A president's principal helpers are his cabinet. The members of Davis's cabinet were for the most part men of less than outstanding ability. The one notable exception was Judah P. Benjamin, but his usefulness was seriously impaired by his extreme unpopularity in Congress, in the army and among some of the leading newspaper men. While Secretary of War, Benjamin antagonized Thomas J. Jackson, Joseph E. Johnston and P. G. T. Beauregard by his tactlessness, and his constant berating of the last two did much to prejudice Davis against them. General Johnston and Senator Wigfall in their war-time correspondence referred to Benjamin as "Jerusalem." Beauregard called him "Mr. Davis's little man Friday." Other prominent Confederates spoke even more disdainfully of him; a Missouri Congressman applied a term to him that is unprintable.

It is generally conceded by authorities on Confederate administration that Secretary of Navy Stephen R. Mallory and Postmaster General John H. Reagan were officials of solid abilities, but their departments were relatively unimportant. Secretary of War James A. Seddon is accorded a high rating by some scholars. He was undoubtedly conscientious and well-meaning, and in the early period of his incumbency showed considerable promise as an administrator. But the burdens of office seemed to stifle his initiative and burn out his energy. On the whole his record appears unimpressive; the same must be said of most of his associates in the Confederate cabinet.

Davis gave his cabinet little opportunity to shine, for he exercised close control over the executive departments. Indeed, his activities extended in some instances to the trivia of internal operations and even to minor appointments in the army. On August 23, 1863, Robert G. H. Kean, Chief of the Bureau of War, entered this damning comment about Davis: "The style of business with which his time is now being consumed is in our present circumstances almost a scandal—little trash which ought to be dispatched by clerks in the Adjt Gen'l's office. This absorption of the Pres'd't's time in trifles (comparative) is due to two facts: 1st, his own desire to be personally conversant about everything; 2nd, the weakness of some the men he has about him, who have accustomed him to have them run to him for instructions about every little matter."

Kean's observations are borne out by similar statements made by Secretary Mallory. "No labours of the War Office were too small for his attention," wrote Mallory shortly after the war. "The amount of attention which he habitually bestowed upon details which are usually devolved upon subordinates surprised all who were familiar with his habits. . . . Letters from afflicted mothers, . . . complaints of friendless soldiers, . . . applications for pardons, . . . petitions from wives for the release of conscripted husbands, or from farmers for the restoration of impressed mules and horses, were in numerous instances read, . . . carefully considered, and responded to by him. . . . A vast amount of such business, which might well have been referred . . . to a Bureau officer . . . encumbered his table and occupied his time."

Both Mallory and Kean testify that Davis was a slow worker. Mallory represents him as dilatory and over-cautious in making decisions, and wasting much time in long-winded discourses. Cabinet meetings, according to Mallory, "occupied from two to five hours, far longer than was required for the thorough examination and [transaction] . . . of current public measures and business; but from his uncontrollable tendency to digression to slide away from chief points to episodical questions, the amount of business bore but little relation to the time consumed."

Davis's prolixity extended in some instances to his

letters, many of which were written in his own hand. One of his missives to Joseph E. Johnston, written shortly after the fall of Vicksburg, ran to fourteen and a half pages. Some of his longer letters, especially those responding to baseless criticism of presidential acts, should not have been written at all.

The enormous amount of time expended by the President on minutiæ might much more appropriately have been devoted to fundamentals of presidential responsibility, such as mapping an overall strategy for winning the war and framing a legislative program for effective utilization of the country's resources. But Davis seemed incapable of thinking in large terms, or of focusing on major problems. Hence the Confederacy drifted from crisis to crisis without benefit of comprehensive political guidance.

* * * * *

A second shortcoming of Davis was his lack of popular appeal. He never developed among the masses that sense of intimacy or identity of interests that distinguishes the master politician. He had none of the common touch of Andrew Jackson or Abraham Lincoln. When Lincoln visited the army, the soldiers hailed him enthusiastically as *their* leader. They regarded him as their protector against the machinations of the speculators and political schemers. In their letters they frequently applied to him such familiar titles as "Old Abe," "Father Abraham" and "Uncle Abe." Davis did not elicit a similar response from Johnny Rebs. In their correspondence they referred to him as the President, and they used the term in a way to suggest more awe than affection. In the thousands of soldier letters that I have read I do not recall having seen such a term as "Uncle Jeff" or "Father Jefferson." Davis did not have the capacity to identify himself with ordinary people.

Even his closest associates seem to have adhered to conventional forms in communicating with Davis. If he had a nickname it fell into disuse before he entered public life.

Sam Houston is said to have referred to the Confederate President as "Jeffy Davis," but the term was one of contempt rather than affection. Houston is also credited with saying that Davis was as ambitious as Lucifer and as cold as a lizard. This characterization was unfair, but there can be no doubt that Davis was deficient in magnetism and that to all save his family and a small circle of intimates, he appeared excessively dignified, aloof and unresponsive. Secretary Mallory who was friendly to the President wrote of him in September, 1865: "Few men could be more chillingly, freezingly cold."

Davis never succeeded in dramatizing the issues of the war nor in arousing the public mind with regard to them. His public statements had nothing of the ringing appeal of a Franklin Roosevelt or a Winston Churchill. His two inaugurals and his addresses to Congress were ably composed, polished pieces, and Davis delivered them in a masterful manner. But a careful analysis of their content reveals serious deficiencies in appeal. He dealt too much in abstractions. His advocacy of the Confederate cause had too much of a negative, defensive quality, stressing unduly the barbarity and the heinousness of the North, and the blindness and obstinacy of foreign nations in failing to align themselves with the South. His speeches also were lacking in realism in that they reflected a degree of optimism unwarranted by circumstances. His intention was doubtless to prevent despondency, and it may well be that his overweening determination for the South to succeed blinded him to the actuality of its deterioration. Whatever his design or conception, the effect of his course was to arouse false hopes that could lead only to bitter disillusionment and lessen the confidence of the people in their President.

If, instead of ignoring realities and dwelling on such negative notes as enemy atrocities, Davis had from the beginning stressed the necessity of enormous sacrifice and pitched the conflict on a high moral plane, his leadership would have been far more effective. Confederates liked to compare their own struggle with the American colonial revolt against England. But Davis was never able to infuse the Southern movement for independence with the lofty purposes and timeless qualities that Jefferson and Paine breathed into the American Revolution.

It has been argued by some that the Southern cause, tied as it was to slavery, did not lend itself to such an idealistic projection—and there can be no doubt that slavery complicated the South's position before the world. But these reservations would not have inhibited Davis in an effort to rally the South to take its stand on lofty principles if he had possessed the necessary attributes for public appeal. As previously observed he himself had no misgivings about slavery and if the South's cause was bad in any other respect he seemed unaware of the fact.

His failure to place the struggle on a high moral level must be attributed largely to his personal qualities. He had not the breadth of vision or the depth of spirit that translates family quarrels into ageless and boundless struggles between tyranny and freedom and right and wrong. He was narrow and legalistic in his thinking and his focus was on the near slope rather than the distant peak.

The restriction of his scope and the legalistic bent of his thought were apparent in his controversies with General Joseph E. Johnston, Governor Zebulon Vance and others. His position was stated with impressive logic, and at great length. But he often seemed more interested in setting the record straight and vindicating his position than in anticipating future problems or effectively solving those at hand. And he sometimes appeared more concerned with winning the argument than promoting the common good.

*　*　*　*　*

Davis was notoriously inept at getting along with people. The patient and long-suffering Seddon remarked to a friend in May, 1864, that "the president was the most difficult man to get along with" he had ever seen. Davis's good friend and consistent champion, Governor Thomas C. Reynolds of Missouri, once admitted to an acquaintance that the President was a man of "marked peculiarities," "stern and unbending" toward his enemies. Even the extremely discreet Lee on one occasion remarked to John B. Gordon: "You know that the President is very pertinacious in opinion and purpose."

In these mild words Lee pointed up one of Davis's greatest weaknesses—namely, a degree of devotion to his own ideas that made him impatient of disagreement. Varina Howell, a remarkably discerning person, sensed this quality in Davis when first she met him. Writing to her mother shortly after being introduced to her future husband, she stated: "He . . . has a way of taking for granted that everybody agrees with him, when he expresses an opinion, which offends me." Later she said of her husband: "He sincerely thought all he said, and moreover could not understand any other man coming to a different conclusion after his premises were stated. It was his sincerity of opinion which sometimes gave him the manner to which his opponents objected as domineering."

Others were less charitable than Mrs. Davis in their appraisal of the President. What she regarded as sincerity and earnestness they were prone to view as opinionatedness and ill-tempered stubbornness. Testimony on this point could be introduced almost without end, but a few random comments will suffice as examples. Stephen R. Mallory once noted in his diary that Davis "wore his personal opinions very openly." W. B. Machen, Confederate Congressman from Kentucky, wrote in April, 1863: "He is inveterately obstinate to a serious fault. It is impossible to correct that fault as it is bred in the bone." James Henry Hammond, distinguished elder statesman of South Carolina, stated to a friend in April, 1861: "He is the most irascible man I ever knew. . . . Quick-tempered, arbitrary, overbearing . . . he is as vain as a peacock [and] as ambitious as the Devil." William Porcher Miles, Chairman of the House Military Affairs Committee, wrote to Beauregard on November 26, 1862: "He cannot brook opposition or criticism, and those who do not *bow down before him* have no chance of success with him."

Miles may have been unduly harsh in his criticism, but there can be no doubt that Davis tended to personalize opposition. Like Woodrow Wilson—and similarities between the two are both numerous and striking—he found it almost impossible to like people who disagreed with him, and antipathies born of opposing opinions often degenerated into bitter quarrels that weakened the administration and injured the Confederacy.

Lincoln made good use in high positions of very difficult persons whom he had every reason to dislike, such as Seward, Chase and Stanton. But Davis had neither the vision nor the bigness to utilize the talents of men who were personally distasteful to him or who staunchly opposed his views.

He was woefully lacking in tact. He knew not how to yield or seem to yield on one front in order to win on another; or to concede a minor point in order to gain a major one. He had not the discernment or temperament that could detect an incipient unpleasantness and prevent its ripening into a formidable antagonism. He never developed the art of permitting an opponent to save his face, of letting him down softly, and of soothing wounds with the oils of sympathy, flattery, cajolery or humor. "Come let us talk it over" were words rarely used by the Confederate President in dealings with refractory cabinet members, legislators or generals.

The fruit of his tactlessness was a host of alienated leaders whose services Davis could ill spare and whose continuing bitterness was extremely damaging to his prestige. Admittedly many with whom Davis quarreled were persons of testy temperament, equally responsible with Davis, if not more so, for the rifts that occurred. But a wiser and greater man than Davis would have prevented some of the strife which crippled Confederate leadership and thus have saved for constructive service some of the capable officials who were estranged from the administrative team.

Secretary of War George W. Randolph is a good case in point. Called to the cabinet from the army in March, 1862, this grandson of Thomas Jefferson was hailed with enthusiasm as the successor of the unpopular Judah P. Benjamin. He applied himself diligently to the duties of his office and did much to improve relations with Congress and the army, which had deteriorated greatly during the incumbency of Benjamin. But he acted with greater independence than his predecessors and eventually took upon himself responsibilities which Davis considered as exclusively his own. In the major issue which led to Randolph's resignation, Davis was clearly right. Randolph, without reference to the President, in November, 1862, ordered General T. H. Holmes at his discretion to cross over the Mississippi from Arkansas with reenforcements and take charge of operations for the defense of Vicksburg. Since the proposal involved the transfer of forces from one military department to another and a change in the command setup, Randolph should not have ordered it without consulting Davis. Randolph modified the orders to Holmes but a subsequent exchange of letters in which Davis stated that "the appointment of commissioned officers is a constitutional function which I have neither power nor will to delegate," led to the Secretary of War's sudden and unconditional resignation.

Had Davis been more tactful he might have forestalled Randolph's resignation. The basic difficulty was the President's unwillingness to concede to his cabinet, and especially to the Secretary of War, any real authority or to take them fully into his counsel. On June 22, 1862, Mallory complained in his diary: "The President does not consult his cabinet either as to plans or arrangement of campaigns, or the appointment of military men to office, & I think he errs in not doing so." And when Randolph resigned Mallory attributed the Secretary's action to "the President's habitual interference in the details of the [War] Department."

Some authorities, leaning heavily on J. B. Jones' *A Rebel War Clerk's Diary,* have belittled Randolph's abilities and accomplishments, but Mallory thought him competent, as did William Porcher Miles, who had frequent dealings with him. When Randolph resigned Miles wrote a friend: "I cannot but regard his retirement . . . as a great public misfortune. He was well-informed, conscientious, upright and laborious. A gentleman of higher tone and character I never met. He was delightful to transact business with—for he was courteous, patient and always perfectly frank and cordial. There was not a particle of indirectness about him. . . . I never hesitated to talk with him in the freest and most confidential manner, and was constantly impressed by the manliness, honesty and purity of his character."

Miles's appraisal may have been colored by his animosity to Davis, but reactions of the press to Randolph's resignation indicate that the country as a whole held a similar view of the secretary's capability, and the President's prestige undoubtedly suffered from his resignation.

In less than a month after Randolph's retirement from the cabinet, Davis had a run-in with Wade Keyes, Assistant Attorney General. In a sharp rebuke of what he regarded an unwarranted criticism of the President's dealings with government accounting officers Davis wrote Keyes: "I do not admit the propriety on the part of a subordinate officer of the government to interpose his criticism on the intercourse between the President and members of the cabinet, especially, if, as in your case, there be no official connection in the matter." Regardless of the merits of the President's position, such a tone was surely not the sort to win friends and influence people.

Even the gentle Lee felt the sting of one of Davis's tactless outbursts. Early in 1865, when Congress was putting pressure on Davis to make Lee general-in-chief, a rumor spread in the Confederate capital that Lee had ordered the destruction of tobacco in the Richmond warehouses. Davis telegraphed Lee to come to the city as he wanted to discuss the situation with him. Lee, deeming it unwise to leave the army at the time, wired back: "Send me the measures and I will send you my views." This response angered the President and led him to send Lee a message closing with these words: "Rest assured I will not ask your views in answer to measures. Your counsels are no longer wanted in this matter." A less generous man than Lee would have taken offense, but "Marse Robert" got on the train, went to Richmond and smoothed the President's ruffled feathers.

* * * * *

Davis's deficiencies in dealing with individuals extended to his relations with his public. He got along poorly with the press, with Congress, with the cabinet and with many of the state officials. E. A. Pollard and J. M. Daniel of the Richmond *Examiner* became his bitter and inveterate enemies, and they with the Rhetts of the Charleston *Mercury* did much to undermine the confidence of the people in the chief executive. Unfortunately, Davis did little to cultivate a friendly press.

The President's relations with Congress deteriorated from almost complete harmony in the beginning to an open conflict that increased in acrimony with the passing of time. Among the opposition were some of the most influential members of the legislative branch, including William Porcher Miles, Chairman of the House Military Affairs Committee, Edward Sparrow, Chairman of the Senate Military Affairs Committee, R. M. T. Hunter, presiding officer of the Senate, Louis T. Wigfall, C. C. Clay and James L. Orr.

Of course some friction between the executive and legislative branches is to be expected, especially in time of war, and more especially when the course of war is unfavorable. Even so, it seems that Davis himself was to blame for much of his difficulty with Congress. In the first place he did not seek actively to ingratiate himself with the legislators. His contacts with them were restricted largely to formal conferences and even these were not as frequent as they might have been. One of the reasons for his inaccessibility was his poor health. On this point Mrs. Davis, in her memoir, makes the following comment: "He was a nervous dyspeptic by habit. . . . He said he could do either one duty or the other—give entertainments or administer the Government—and he fancied he was expected to perform the latter service in preference; and so we ceased to entertain, except at formal receptions or informal dinners and breakfasts given to as many as Mr. Davis's health permitted us to invite. . . . In the evening he was too exhausted to receive informal visitors." "It would have been much better," she continued, "if the

President could have met the Congress, and the State officials as well as the citizens socially and often, for the magnetism of his personality would have greatly mollified their resentments."

Mrs. Davis was unquestionably right about Davis's ability, when he chose, to leave a good impression on those to whom he played host. In his home his dignity, poise, gracious manner, and informed conversation, were utilized to best advantage and the effects on his visitors were most favorable. Colonel Arthur Fremantle wrote after a tea at the Davis mansion on June 17, 1863: "Nothing can exceed the charm of his manner, which is simple, easy and most fascinating. . . . I don't think it is possible for anyone to have an interview with him without going away most favorably impressed by his agreeable, unassuming manner, and by the charm of his conversation."

Warren Akin, a Congressman from Georgia, received a similar impression when he called on Davis early in 1865. After the visit Akin wrote his wife: "I had a long conversation with the President yesterday. He has been greatly wronged. . . . [He] is not that stern, puffed up man he is represented to be. He was polite, attentive and as communicative with me as I could wish. . . . He was very cordial in his reception of me, and in his invitation to me to call again."

Not all Congressmen who visited Davis came away as favorably disposed as Akin. When R. M. T. Hunter, presiding officer of the Confederate Senate, went to see the President in December, 1863, to talk over some important legislation, Davis launched into a denunciation of Virginia, the visitor's home state, and Hunter was so affronted that he departed without ever mentioning the business which prompted his call.

This episode, while most unfortunate in view of Hunter's position and influence, should not obscure the basic fact of the President's potential charm. And his ability to make a favorable impression was not confined to individual relationships. Private correspondence and press reports indicate that when Davis appealed directly to the people in public address the results were beneficial. On October 7, 1864, a Georgia editor wrote the President: "Your visit to this section of our country has been productive of much good. Your speeches along the route have been eagerly read and pondered; and their hopeful, confident tone has had a great effect. . . . Your remarks have . . . tended to cheer the despondent and strengthen the weak." How unfortunate for Davis and the Confederate cause that he appeared before his constituents so infrequently. He left the environs of Richmond only three times, and the purpose of these trips was more to explore the military situation than raise the spirits of his people.

The truth of the matter seems to be that Davis neither realized the importance of cultivating good will nor was he willing to pay the price of being a popular leader. In his rise to political eminence, he had never had to struggle for public favor. The powerful influence of his brother Joe was in large measure responsible for his initial political success, election to Congress in 1845. The only other public office to which he was elected before becoming Confederate President was the United States Senate and Senators were chosen not by the people, but by the state legislature. He became Provisional President of the Confederacy by vote of a small group at Montgomery and he was elected permanent president without opposition.

The marked contrast of Davis's political career with that of Lincoln is immediately apparent. The Union President had started at the bottom of the political ladder and had fought his way to the top against stiff opposition. He had had to appeal directly to the people all along the way. He had been compelled to master the game of politics at every level. Davis skipped the lower rungs of the ladder and felt relatively little need of keeping in close touch with the masses or cultivating the elementary arts of political maneuver. He seemed to consider himself above the rough and tumble activities of the smoke filled room.

Because he did not feel it necessary to curry public favor, and because he had a distaste for social intermingling, he developed habits of aloofness that were to prove a great handicap to him when he became leader of the Lost Cause.

In her reminiscences Mrs. Davis recalled that while her husband was Senator, he devoted little time to society. "He was so impervious to the influence of anything but principle in shaping his political course," she stated, "that he underrated the effect of social intercourse in determining the action of public men and never sought to exert it in behalf of his own policy. In consequence we went out but little, and spent our evenings together."

This aloofness from fellow politicians was continued in the Confederate White House. Secretary Mallory, while confined at Fort Lafayette in September, 1865, made this astute observation: "[Davis's] relations with members of Congress were not what they should have been; nor

were they what they might have been. . . . Position &
opportunity presented him every means of cultivating the
personal good will of members by little acts of attention,
courtesy or deference, which no man, however high his
position, who has to work by means of his fellows, can
dispense with. . . . While he was ever frank & cordial to
his friends & those whose conduct he approved, he would
not &, I think, could not, sacrifice a smile, an inflexion
of the voice, or a demonstration of attention to flatter the
self-love of any who did not stand well in his esteem.
. . . By members of Congress, who had to see him on business, his manners to, & reception of them were frequently
complained of & pronounced ungracious & irritable. . . .
Though he listened patiently, & heard all they had to say
. . . & in return calmly & precisely stated his reasons
against the [proposed] measure, he rarely satisfied or
convinced them simply because in his manner & language
there was just an indescribable something which offended
their self-esteem & left their judgements room to find
fault with him. Some of his best friends left him at times
with feelings bordering closely upon anger . . . and with
a determination hastily formed, of calling no more upon
him; & many of them embracing some of the most sen-
sible, prudent, calm & patriotic men of both houses, were
alienated from him more or less from this cause. It was
of no use for his friends . . . to counsel him to adopt a
different manner toward the members of Congress & to
see them sociably &c; for he could not do this; it was not
in his nature, & his restless, manly, open & turbulent spirit
turned from what to him was the faintest approach to
seek popularity; & he scorned to believe it necessary to

coax men to do their duty in the then condition of their country."

While Davis unquestionably was hampered greatly by neuralgia, eye-strain, nervous indigestion and insomnia during his days in the Confederate White House, his lack of sociableness cannot be attributed to poor health alone. The President found time for many things that he wanted to do. Certainly some of the innumerable hours that he devoted to administrative details might more profitably have been given to public relations.

A considerable factor in the President's unpopularity with Congress and with the country at large was his persistent support of discredited officials. Unfortunately some of those to whom he clung most tenaciously were men of mediocre abilities while others were grossly incompetent. Lucius B. Northrop, the Confederate Commissary General, was, to say the least, not such a brilliant success as to be indispensable. Many leaders in the army, in Congress and in the country at large came to regard him as hopelessly inefficient. But Davis had taken a stand for Northrop in the pre-war period, and he refused to heed the mounting criticism of him during the conflict. On January 18, 1865, J. B. Jones noted in his diary that Northrop was "still held by the President, contrary to the wishes of the whole Confederacy." Not until February, 1865, after the Confederate House of Representatives specifically demanded Northrop's dismissal, did Davis remove him. And he continued to defend him long after the clash of arms had ceased.

Confederate Senator W. S. Oldham wrote shortly after the war that "the attachment of President Davis to such generals as Bragg, Pemberton and Holmes seemed to amount almost to infatuation, and appeared to increase as the confidence of the country in them died out, and he could never be induced to relieve them from command until after they had inflicted irreparable damage on our cause." Davis's defense of Pemberton can be justified to some extent on the ground that the President was largely to blame for his being bottled up at Vicksburg. But his course with reference to Bragg cannot be sustained on any reasonable ground. Bragg proved his gross incompetency as a high commander on the Kentucky campaign; further evidence of his incapacity was afforded by Murfreesboro and Chickamauga; and Missionary Ridge gave crowning proof of his inability to lead an army in combat. But Davis apparently remained blind to Bragg's deficiencies. The basis of the President's attitude is suggested by a letter he wrote to Bragg on August 5, 1862, in which he remarked: "You have the misfortune of being regarded as my personal friend, and one pursued therefore with malignant censure by men regardless of truth."

So, interpreting criticisms of Bragg as attacks on himself, he held him in command in the face of the bitterest and most widespread opposition, and when finally compelled to let him go, brought him to Richmond and made him his chief military adviser. Thus did a discredited and despised general become the President's go-between with Congress and the cabinet and his spokesman in dealings with field commanders. Never did a chief executive make a more tactless appointment! That Davis was still clinging to Bragg as the Confederacy crumbled about him is indicated by a letter written to him by his wife as she fled southward on April 7, 1865. "The way things look now, the trans Miss seems our ultimate destination," she stated. "Though I know you do not like my interference, let me entreat you not to send B. B. to command there. I am satisfied that the country will be ruined by its infestive feuds if you do so. . . . Even those who hope for favors in that event deprecate it for you."

Davis incurred almost as much hostility for opposing persons popular with the country and Congress as he did for preferring his own favorites. His removal of Beauregard in 1862, and especially the manner in which he did it, provoked a flood of protest. While the Army of Tennessee was at Tupelo, in June, 1862, Beauregard, who was ailing, turned the command temporarily over to Bragg, the next ranking officer, and on his surgeon's certificate of disability went to Bladon Springs, Alabama, to recuperate. He did not obtain prior authority from the War Department but on June 14 telegraphed Adjutant General Cooper of his intentions. On the same day, June 14, Davis wired Bragg to proceed to Jackson, Mississippi, to take command temporarily of General Mansfield Lovell's department; his message closed with the words: "The necessity is urgent and absolute." On June 14, also, Davis sent his aide, William Preston Johnston, to Tupelo on an inspection trip, with instructions that indicated dissatisfaction with Beauregard's recent retrograde movement and other activities in the exercise of command. When later Davis was informed of Beauregard's unauthorized departure for Alabama, he was furious. On June 20 he sent Bragg a telegram assigning Bragg permanently to the command of the Army of Tennessee.

Beauregard was undoubtedly at fault in taking leave of his army without first clearing with his superiors. But in view of the fact that his health was poor, that his absence was to be only temporary, that the military situation was quiescent, and that he could be reached by telegraph in case of emergency, Davis's abrupt removal of him from command seems unjustifiable. The conclusion is inescapable that Davis welcomed a pretext for replacing him with Bragg.

Whatever the thoughts behind the action, the consequences in terms of public relations were most unfortunate. Beauregard was still the hero of Sumter and Manassas, and he had many friends in high places. The "Grand Creole" could not be so unceremoniously laid on the shelf, without a kick-back from his admirers.

On September 13, 1862, Senators Edward Sparrow and Thomas Semmes of Louisiana presented to the President a paper signed by fifty-nine Senators and Representatives, protesting Beauregard's removal and petitioning his restoration to command of the Army of Tennessee. Semmes' notes on the interview represent Davis as saying "that so far as giving Beauregard command of Bragg's Army is concerned, that was out of the question. Bragg had arranged all his plans . . . and to put a new commander at the head of the army would be so prejudicial to the public interests, he would not do it if the whole world united in the petition."

The petitioners, among whom were some of the most powerful men in Congress, were, to say the least, not soothed by the President's uncompromising rejoinder. Not long afterward the petition, along with Semmes' notes on the interview and other papers, was printed. The circulation of this pamphlet could only have increased the damage to Davis's prestige. On many this incident must have left the impression that Davis had taken unfair advantage of a sick hero, whom he disliked, to supplant him with one of his own pets.

Congress was also greatly annoyed by the President's conduct toward Quartermaster General A. C. Myers. Myers had served with distinction in the Mexican War and in 1848 was quartermaster general of the Army of Mexico. On March 25, 1861, he was appointed acting Quartermaster General of the Confederacy and within a year was elevated to the position of Quartermaster General and promoted to colonel. Then, for some reason, he fell into disfavor with Davis. A report was circulated in the War Department which placed the blame on Mrs. Myers. According to this report Mrs. Myers at a dinner party referred to Mrs. Davis as an old squaw, because of her dark complexion, and the incident was reported to the President. Be that as it may, when Congress in an effort to obtain Myers's promotion specified the grade of brigadier for his position, Davis on August 7, 1863, appointed Brigadier General Alexander R. Lawton Quartermaster General. Myers's friends in Congress were much offended. Senator Wigfall denounced the President's act as "petty tyranny, reckless disregard of law and contemptuous treatment of Congress," an example of "his bad passions & miserable malignancy toward individuals." The Senate registered a formal protest on January 26, 1864, but to no avail. Myers, refusing to serve under Lawton, left Confederate service.

Even more costly to Davis's standing with Congress and the country was his controversy with General Joseph E. Johnston. There was right and wrong on both sides in this quarrel, and the issues are too involved to permit of detailed examination here. But whatever Johnston's faults, he was respected by his fellow generals, beloved by his soldiers, stood high in public esteem and had ardent supporters in Congress. As in the case of Beauregard, Davis erred in his manner of dealing with Johnston and his maladroitness was partly responsible for deterioration of relations between the two from minor disagreements to impassioned quarrels which rocked the whole Confederacy. Davis was surely culpable in assigning and holding Johnston after his recovery from the Fair Oaks' wound to a position in the West which the general did not want and which he repeatedly declared impracticable. And it is difficult to imagine a greater indiscretion than sending Bragg, who had consistently failed as army commander, to Georgia in July, 1864, to confer with Johnston about his plans and to pass on that leader's success.

Whatever the justification of the President's treatment of Johnston, there can be no doubt that one result of the controversy was to nourish the impression that Davis placed personal animus above public weal.

* * * * *

Another of Davis's shortcomings as President was neglect of civil functions in favor of military matters. As previously noted, if he could have had the decision he would have become military commander instead of chief executive. This initial hankering for field command persisted. On May 10, 1861, Mrs. Davis wrote Senator C. C. Clay from Montgomery: "There is a good deal of talk here of his going to Richmond as commander of the forces. I hope it may be done, for to him military command is a perfect system of hygiene." Writing after the war of the situation in the summer of 1863 she stated:

"The President was a prey to the acutest anxiety during this period, and again and again said: If I could take one wing and Lee the other, I think we could between us wrest a victory from those people." (If she had realized the unwarranted presumption behind the statement she surely would not have quoted it. What right had he who had led only a regiment in the Mexican War to put himself on the same basis with a man who had commanded an army in such brilliant victories as Second Manassas and Chancellorsville!). Again, referring to the campaigns of 1864, she said: "After the army fell back to Petersburg, he looked forward to personally taking command in the West, and cooperating with General Lee in one great battle, which he hoped to be decisive."

Even more revealing was a statement that Winnie Davis made about her father in 1895. "He, my mother and I were sitting together one spring evening at Beauvoir," she wrote. "I asked him if he would have his life to live over again what he would best like to be. He turned to me and I could see his blue eyes shine in the gloaming with the light of other days as he answered without a moment's hesitation, 'I would be a cavalry officer and break squares.' His love of the army lay in the warmest corner of his heart."

This deep-seated fondness for the military and a dislike of political administration caused him to devote disproportionate attention to the former. His personal and official correspondence reveal a far greater concern about what went on in the army than about the state of the country and the administration of the government. True, the two were inseparable, and in a nation at war the armed services are a matter of paramount concern.

But the Confederacy was relatively well-off with respect to military command. Its crying need was for political guidance; for a dynamic leadership that would draw its discordant elements together and make available for effective use the last ounce of its limited manpower and material strength. Unfortunately for the South and for its President, Davis chose to concentrate his attention and energy in the area of lesser need.

He wrote unnecessary and lengthy letters to army subordinates; he consumed a vast amount of time in passing on minor military appointments; he kept a sharp eye on the details of military legislation; his messages to congress stressed the military situation and devoted far too little attention to such vital problems as finance. In the summer of 1862 and again in 1864, when Congress was in rebellious mood and civil affairs urgently demanded his attention, Davis rode frequently to the battlefield where he was not needed, and indeed where his presence caused anxiety and embarrassment for the army commander. On these visits, according to Mrs. Davis, "the President . . . bitterly regretted his executive office and longed to engage actively in the fight."

She was right in her prior statement about the hygienic effects of the army on her husband. During periods when remoteness of the armies from Richmond or the pressure of administrative duties prevented visits to the field, Davis's health deteriorated. But when he was in frequent and intimate contact with the army, even on a strenuous tour such as that which took him to Tennessee and Mississippi in 1862, his physical condition improved. The insomnia and throbbing nerves about which Mrs. Davis spoke so often came after days in the office and not after visits to Lee's headquarters when Richmond seemed in peril. The inescapable conclusion is that civil administration was irksome to Davis and that military activity was pleasant.

Davis's over-concentration on military affairs might have been less tragic had he been more effective in his constitutional role of commander-in-chief. But his performance in that capacity left much to be desired. A basic shortcoming of course was his failure to map an overall strategy for bringing to bear the full weight of the Confederacy's military might against the Union. Closely related to this deficiency was the failure until Congress forced his hand near the end of the war to unify the Confederate command under a general-in-chief. On July 12, 1863, Robert Kean noted in his diary: "The Radical vice of Mr. Davis' whole military system is the separate departmental organization—each reporting only to him. It makes each Department depend only on its *own* strength and deprives them of the mutual support and combination which might else be obtained." As Kean aptly observed, the system which held the forces east and west of the Mississippi within boundaries that could be crossed only by the direct authorization of the President contributed to the disastrous loss of Vicksburg and Port Hudson.

Davis made a gesture toward unification of command under Lee in 1862, but as Douglas S. Freeman has plainly shown, Lee was general-in-chief in name only. Davis kept in his own hand the making of major decisions and the actual direction of military affairs.

Study of Davis's orders and correspondence indicates that throughout the war he descended from the high level of broad policy to that of field operations and departmental administration. To the extent that he entered these areas of activity he departed from the rightful role of commander-in-chief and dissipated energies that should have been reserved for matters of fundamental moment.

* * * * *

Perhaps the greatest of all Davis's shortcomings was his lack of capacity for growth. Lord Charnwood, the distinguished English biographer, said of Lincoln: "The exercise of power and the endurance of responsibility gave him new strength. . . . The man grew to his task. . . . [He was] a man who started by being tough and shrewd and canny and became very strong and very wise, started with inclination to honesty, courage and kindness, and became under a tremendous strain, honest, brave and kind to an almost tremendous degree."

At the outset of their presidential careers Davis seemed clearly to have the edge on Lincoln. He was better educated, had a much greater knowledge of military matters, was far more experienced in high-level politics and public administration, and enjoyed enormous social and economic advantages. In his early days in the White House Lincoln appeared awkward and uncertain and lacked the confidence of many of the national leaders. Davis on the other hand seemed poised and certain and had the respect of the South's dominant figures. But in the crisis of war Lincoln grew in wisdom, in spirit and in the affection of his people, while Davis followed an opposite course. Under the burdens of the Confederate presidency—and unquestionably they were enormous—Davis fretted about his problems, fought back at his opponents, shrivelled in spirit and declined in public esteem.

Only in the after years did Davis reveal the full measure of his better self. Defeat and imprisonment had a chastening effect on him. The Southern people, likewise humbled by surrender and its consequences, turned from denouncing their former chieftain and began to hail him as the martyr of the Lost Cause. Under the spell of their commiseration and affection, Davis became warm and gentle. His health grew better and even his eyesight improved. Indeed, he became a new man. Spiritually and physically his last years were his best years. In defeat and old age he was able to achieve that which had been denied him while President of the Confederacy—peace with himself and his fellow man.

A few months after Appomattox Davis wrote his wife: "That power to compare and sift testimony is as necessary to a historian as to an attorney." The foregoing appraisal, though it represents the effort of a historian to weigh the evidence and to strike a fair balance may seem to the admirers of Davis to be unduly harsh. It is a judgment on the man as President, focused on his years in the Confederate White House when he was put to his severest public test and appeared at his worst. His position as Confederate President was most difficult, and any mortal who occupied it would have been sorely tried and severely criticized. But the outcome of the test makes it hard not to conclude that he was ill-fitted for the responsibilities of the office, that he should not have accepted it and that some other Southerner could have done the job better than he.

James Redpath once observed that there were two

Jefferson Davises. He was referring to the despised traitor known in the North and the beloved Southern patriarch whom he came to know intimately during a lengthy visit at Beauvoir after the war. But there were also two Davises during the period of the Confederacy. One was a warm, understanding and affectionate father, husband and friend; the other was a cold, stubborn and unapproachable administrator. One was a modest, idealistic and dedicated statesman; the other was an opinionated, short-sighted and imperious public official. One was a well-meaning, long-suffering and consecrated leader; the other was a petty, contentious and presumptuous chieftain. The nobler of these two Davises was the one remembered by his admirers, the other was the man as he appeared to his enemies. To the historian who attempts to judge him in the perspective of time both the virtues and the faults are apparent, but his record as President leaves more to condemn than to praise.

THE ROAD TO APPOMATTOX

Century Magazine, June 1887

Jefferson Davis—*The Reluctant Helmsman*

Photograph by Brady

Courtesy National Archives

Inauguration of Davis at Montgomery,
February 18, 1861

Courtesy National Archives

Confederate Leaders with whom Davis Quarreled

Robert Barnwell Rhett, member of Confederate Provisional Congress from South Carolina and editor, with his son, of the Charleston Mercury, Anti-Davis newspaper.

← *Courtesy Frederick H. Meserve*

Robert Barnwell Rhett, Jr., editor, with his father, of the Charleston Mercury. ⟫→

Courtesy Frederick H. Meserve

Left—William Porcher Miles, Anti-Davis leader in Confederate Congress and chairman of the House Military Affairs Committee.

↓ Photograph by Brady—*Courtesy National Archives*

Center—Louis T. Wigfall, powerful Anti-Davis leader in Confederate Senate, from Texas. ↑

Courtesy Frederick H. Meserve

Right—George W. Randolph of Virginia, Confederate Secretary of War who resigned after a verbal clash with Jefferson Davis in the fall of 1862. ↑

Courtesy Frederick H. Meserve

Robert Toombs, First Confederate Secretary of State, Brigadier General in the Confederate Army, vehement enemy of Davis.

Photograph by Brady

Courtesy National Archives

General Joseph E. Johnston, Confederate Army. His feud with Davis began early in the war, raged throughout the conflict and continued long after Appomattox.

Photograph by Brady

Courtesy National Archives

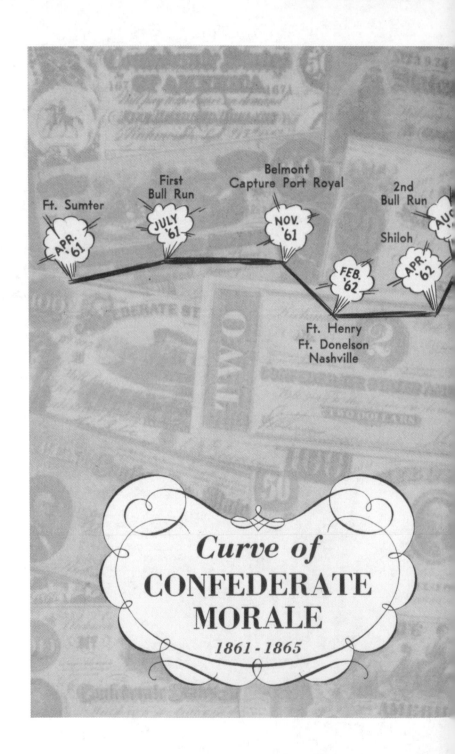

Ft. Sumter

APR. '61

First Bull Run

JULY '61

Belmont Capture Port Royal

NOV. '61

FEB. '62

Ft. Henry
Ft. Donelson
Nashville

2nd Bull Run

AUG

Shiloh

APR. '62

Curve of
CONFEDERATE MORALE
1861 - 1865

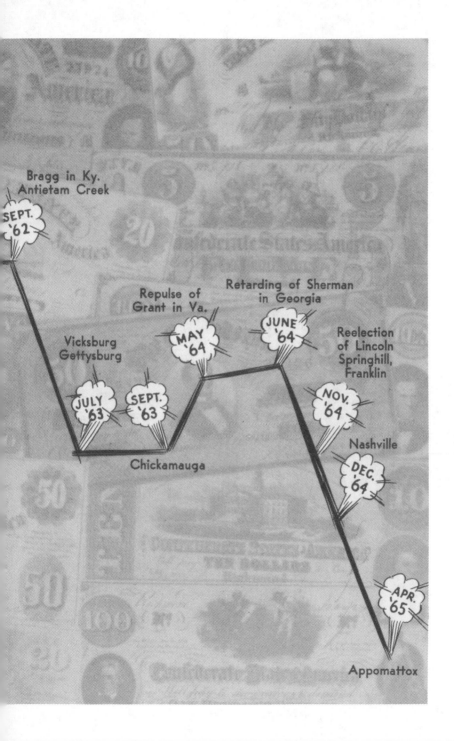

General Robert E. Lee
at home after Appomattox
Photograph by Brady
Courtesy National Archives

General U. S. Grant
on a reconnoitering mission at Spottsylvania,
May 1864

From a war-time sketch made by C. W. Reed,
Century Magazine, June 1887

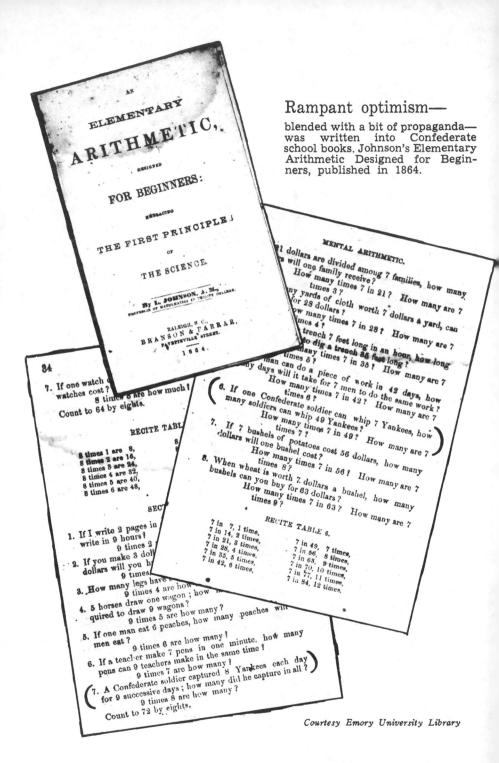

Rampant optimism—

blended with a bit of propaganda—was written into Confederate school books. Johnson's Elementary Arithmetic Designed for Beginners, published in 1864.

The Surrender at Appomattox as portrayed by artist Alonzo Chappel.
Courtesy National Archives

The McLean House at Appomattox.
Photograph by Brady—*Courtesy National Archives*

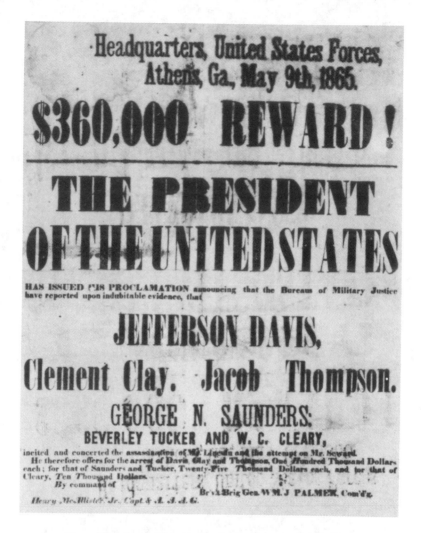

Headquarters, United States Forces, Athens, Ga., May 9th, 1865.

$360,000 REWARD!

THE PRESIDENT OF THE UNITED STATES

HAS ISSUED HIS PROCLAMATION announcing that the Bureau of Military Justice have reported upon indubitable evidence, that

JEFFERSON DAVIS,
Clement Clay. Jacob Thompson.
GEORGE N. SAUNDERS:
BEVERLEY TUCKER AND W. C. CLEARY,

incited and concerted the assassination of Mr. Lincoln and the attempt on Mr. Seward. He therefore offers for the arrest of Davis, Clay and Thompson, One Hundred Thousand Dollars each; for that of Saunders and Tucker, Twenty-Five Thousand Dollars each, and for that of Cleary, Ten Thousand Dollars.

By command of

Brvt Brig Gen. WM. J PALMER, Com'd'g.

Henry McAllister, Jr. Capt. & A. A. A. G.

Broadside issued by Federals in May, 1865, offering reward for arrest of Jefferson Davis and other Confederate leaders charged with complicity in Lincoln's assassination.

Chapter 2   THE WANING OF
THE SOUTHERN WILL

N JANUARY, 1864, Alexander H. Stephens, Vice-President of the Confederacy, wrote Jefferson Davis: "The greatest and last hope [of the South] is in the willing hearts of the people." Earlier in the conflict Davis himself had made an almost identical statement. A recent history of the Confederacy, by E. Merton Coulter, one of the ablest authorities in the field, states that the cause of the South's failure to achieve independence may be summed up in the fact that "the people did not will hard enough and long enough to win."

What can the historian say of the vicissitudes of Confederate morale and patterns in its manifestations?

Southern morale was exceedingly high at the beginning of the conflict. Indeed, it is doubtful that any people ever went to war with greater enthusiasm than did Confederates in 1861.

South Carolina's withdrawal from the Union was

43

greeted with tumultuous displays of enthusiasm throughout the lower South. A Texan who was visiting in New Orleans when news arrived that the Palmetto State had seceded wrote to his mother: "Such a row I never witnessed before. One would have thought that the *Messiah* had come surely. . . . The cannon were firing almost all day long . . . and the Pelican flag (a new institution and device) was raised amidst much rejoicing." A similar round of celebrations accompanied the secession of each of the other states.

Long before the shooting started Memphis girls began to don calico and give "hard times" parties as an evidence of their patriotism, while elsewhere in the South women retrieved looms and spinning wheels from attics and closets, and produced Confederate homespun to prove their independence of Yankee fads and factories. In March, 1861, more than a month before their state seceded, students of the University of Virginia raised the Confederate flag on the campus to the stirring strains of "Dixie" and fired a salute to celebrate the occasion.

Fort Sumter and the call to arms raised Southern spirit to flood tide. Unionists, cooperationists and moderates of all shades and persuasions were swamped by the mighty wave. Resistance to the raging war fervor was futile; and in some sections it was dangerous.

The eagerness of all types and classes of people to have a part in the struggle was demonstrated in letters written to the governor of Virginia. One man wrote: "As we are about to have a brush with the Northern barbarians I wish to be counted in." A venerable citizen who had already sent five sons and a Negro servant to camp informed the chief executive: "I have but one single daughter and she desires me to say to your Exc. that if you will furnish her with *Suitable Arms* she will undertake deeds of daring that will astonish many of the sterner sex. And if these with their Gallant Officers & Comrades are not enough to satisfy *Northern Averice and fanaticism,* you can have the remaining strength of your most obt Servant, Thos. G. Spencer." An Albermarle County resident wrote the governor that "All of us are . . . ripe and ready for the fight. . . . I shall be shoulder to shoulder with you when ever the fight comes off. I go for taking Boston & Cincinati. I go for wipeing them out." And a Loudoun Countian stated that: "I feel as if I could whip or hurt four Yankeys."

The rampant optimism—blended with a bit of propaganda—was written into Confederate school books. Johnson's *Elementary Arithmetic Designed for Beginners,* published in 1864, but reflecting the sentiment of earlier times, set forth for solution by young Rebels the following problems: (1) "A Confederate soldier captured 8 Yankees each day for 9 successive days; how many did he capture in all?" (2) "If one Confederate soldier kill 90 yankees, how many yankees can 10 Confederate soldiers kill?" (3) "If one Confederate soldier can whip 7 Yankees, how many soldiers can whip 49 Yankees?"

Everywhere state and Confederate authorities were overwhelmed in the spring and summer of 1861 by proffers of service. Martial ardor was especially great in the deep South. The fighting fever invaded school rooms and college halls and in some instances swept away to camp both faculty and students. The tug of war pulled mightily at feminine hearts, and had authorities only given the nod a host of Rebel "Wacs" would proudly have taken their places beside the Southern men. On May 10, 1861, a Georgia woman wrote: "We have formed a Female Company in Bascom for the purpose of learning to shoot, so that if all the men go to war we can protect our homes and selves. . . . The name of our Company is the Bascom Home Guards. You know how nervous and timid Mollie was. Well now she can load a gun and fire and hit a spot at a good distance. . . . We are all delighted with the idea of learning to shoot. Father says he thinks our uniform is prettier than the boys although ours are made of common calico."

Records do not reveal whether or not the patriotic members of the Bascom Home Guard ever had an opportunity to employ their shooting skill. But it is known that the martial urge became so strong among a few Confederate women as to impel them to disguise themselves as men and essay the role of fighters.

As they girded themselves for war most Southerners seemed to anticipate a quick and easy victory. Fire-eating orators, reckless editors and street-corner patriots confidently predicted that the North would never cross swords with the South; and if war perchance should come, they boasted, one brave and chivalrous Southerner could put to flight several of the craven mudsills who comprised the bulk of the Yankee population. Even as well-informed a Confederate as James H. Hammond wrote in early July, 1861: "Our universal belief is that we can . . . [whip them on an open field] one to two and we have no officer who would not be disgraced by retreating if he had one to three."

The first big battle on July 21, 1861, at Manassas

tended to confirm these ideas of Southern fighting superiority. In an editorial of September 27, 1861, John M. Daniel of the Richmond *Examiner* gloated: "The battle of Manassas demonstrated, at once and forever, the superiority of the Southern soldiers, and there is not a man in the army, from the humblest private to the highest officer, who does not feel it. . . . The enemy . . . know now that when they go forth to the field they will encounter a master race. The consciousness of this fact will cause their knees to tremble beneath them on the day of battle. It will demoralize them. It has already done so."

Rebel troops who were not in the first Manassas engagement feared that they would never get a chance to meet the Yankees. Many who held these apprehensions were to die of Federal bullets.

The opportunity to fight did not come immediately, for after Bull Run the North had to build up its strength; and difficulties of supply and a critical shortage of arms prevented the South from following up the advantage gained on the plains of Manassas. During the final months of 1861, Southern ardor cooled perceptibly. The rush to arms that had swept over the country like a tidal wave in the spring and summer dwindled to a trickle or ceased altogether. In November, 1861, the officer in charge of mustering recruits in South Carolina wrote from Columbia: "[My job] is a sinecure because there are no troops coming in although near twenty days have elapsed since 'South Carolina's soil is desecrated'—the deep-mouthed curse, the fierce shout, the wild rush to arms and vengeance—aint here." On Christmas day General Albert Sidney Johnston who was trying desperately to build up the long thin line of defense extending from Columbus, Kentucky to Cumberland Gap wrote to Governor Isham G. Harris of Tennessee: "Ten or fifteen thousand additional troops would make me feel assured of victory. . . . For the last four months, I have endeavored to obtain additional forces from Tennessee and other states, but notwithstanding the efforts of your Excellency and other Governors, the response has been feeble and the forces inadequate to the momentary interests involved."

Correspondence of Confederate governors preserved in state archives afford striking evidence of the declining zeal. Incoming files for the months of April, May, June and July, 1861, are fat with eager offers to enlist and importunate requests for authority to raise companies and regiments. Folders for August and September are much less bulky, and by the end of the year they are in marked contrast to their thick companions of the spring and summer.

The ebbing of zeal was apparent in Confederate camps. In September, 1861, a Louisiana private wrote from a training center near New Orleans: "how I wish this war was over, there ain't a bit of fun in it." About the same time an Alabamian stationed near Manassas wrote to his civilian brother: "I will stay here until about the middle of December then if you will take my place I will come home. . . . I know . . . you feel that you ought to be fighting for your country. So did I, but 3 months service has completely cooled my patriotism. . . . I would advise you to stay at home for the present."

Many other Rebs registered similar opinions, and their statements were confirmed by comments of officers.

In October, 1861, Major General Will T. Martin wrote from Centerville, Virginia, that dissatisfaction and discouragement were widespread in the Army of Northern Virginia. "The first flush of patriotism led many a man to join who now regrets it," he stated, "and they are beginning to resort to all sorts of means to get home."

Patriotism continued to decline throughout the winter, at home and in the army, and in the spring as the war moved into its second year, the Confederacy faced its first great crisis of morale.

* * * * *

A principal cause of this crisis was an unfavorable turn in the South's military fortunes. The thumping victories on Bull Run in July and Wilson's Creek in August marked the peaks of Confederate success in 1861. With the seizure of Port Royal Harbor in South Carolina in November the Federals initiated a series of coastal victories which by mid-May of 1862 had brought into their possession Roanoke Island, New Bern, and Fort Macon, North Carolina, Fort Pulaski, Georgia, and Pensacola, Florida. These triumphs bit off valuable hunks of Southern territory and posed a serious threat to the Confederacy's foreign trade. In March, 1862, General Joseph E. Johnston fell back from Centerville, Virginia, leaving behind badly needed supplies and equipment, and in the same month McClellan launched his "on to Richmond" move by way of the Virginia peninsula.

In the West, Confederates experienced far more serious setbacks. The loss of Fort Henry and Fort Donelson in February, 1862, along with some fifteen thousand men and vast quantities of precious firearms, was a crippling blow. It led to the evacuation of Nashville, first of the state capitals to fall into Federal possession, set on the road to success the Union leader who at Donelson won the title of "Unconditional Surrender" Grant and gave the invaders control of rivers that flowed into the Southern heartland. Confederates suffered another serious defeat at Shiloh on April 6 and 7, lost New Orleans late in the same month and yielded Memphis on June 6. Meanwhile, March 6-8, Federal forces west of the Mississippi won a decisive victory at Pea Ridge, Arkansas, which established Union control of Missouri for the remainder of the war.

The depressing effect of these reverses on the public mind found expression in numerous letters and diaries. On March 1, 1862, a Louisiana girl noted in her journal: "February has been a month of defeats—Roanoke Island, Forts Henry and Donelson, and now proud old Nashville. All have fallen. A bitter month for us." About the same time the erudite and sophisticated William H. Trescot of South Carolina wrote to Congressman William Porcher Miles: "I hear there is some talk of evacuating Wilmington. . . . This perpetual evacuation will become a chronic dysentery under which the strongest constitution would perish. Can't we hold something?" On April 26, 1862, Mary Boykin Chesnut noted in her diary: "Telegrams say the mortar fleet has passed the forts at New Orleans. Down into the very depth of despair go we." The next day she wrote: "New Orleans is gone, and with it the Confederacy."

The gloom produced by Northern victories permeated all classes and groups, except confirmed Unionists and slaves. The Negroes rejoiced in reverse measure to their owners' dejection, though they discreetly concealed their satisfaction save in areas where the actual presence of the invaders gave them protection.

Among Southern leaders who registered depression was William L. Yancey who on March 14, 1862, wrote Senator C. C. Clay that Federal success at New Orleans "would be the knell of our cause in Europe and perhaps on this continent." A month later Herschel V. Johnson wrote to Alexander H. Stephens: "I cant tell you half how despondent I am. If you have words of encouragement founded on reasonable data, I wish to hear them."

A second influence contributing to the morale crisis of 1862 was the hardship which accompanied the war and which by the end of the first year was bearing heavily on many Southern homes. The flood of volunteering that followed Fort Sumter disrupted farm operations and deprived numerous families of their principal means of support. Economic disequilibrium resulting from secession and mobilization combined with a shortage of money to produce business stagnation in towns and cities. Issuance of local scrip and Confederate notes eased the currency situation in the latter part of 1861, but the benefits were offset by the increase in prices which came from depreciation of money and the scarcity created by military needs and the tightening of the blockade. In August, 1861, a visitor to Memphis wrote in his diary that the city was "rather dull for this Season. No prospect for any cotton Season while the blockade lasts, and consequently a general depression of business." In Memphis, and in the Confederacy as a whole, conditions grew worse with the passing of time and by the spring of 1862 many Southerners were hungry, ragged and discouraged.

An example of conditions and attitudes existent in

many localities is afforded by a letter of a plain Georgia woman to her soldier brother on February 17, 1862. "It is the hardeste times in olde Cobb I ever Saw," she stated, "lyeing, Swindling and a Speculation is all that is goinge on here now. thare is littel Sade about war here all that has the means to go on is a trying to Seake and devour evry thing."

The folk at home could have borne their hardship in better spirit if their minds had been at ease about loved ones in the army. But letters from camp in the summer and autumn of 1861 brought distressing reports of sickness and inadequate medical care, followed in numerous instances by sad tidings of death. With the approach of winter, anxieties increased because of the added hazards and discomforts that came with the season.

Among both civilians and soldiers the thing that did most to sustain morale during the first months of the conflict was the conviction that the war would soon end and families be reunited. But events of early 1862 greatly impaired this hope. Far from giving up the struggle, the North manifestly was pressing ahead with increased vigor. Fort Donelson and Pea Ridge gave undeniable proof that not all Yankees were cowards. And the Confederacy's resort to conscription in April, 1862, blasted prospects of an early return of Johnny Rebs to their homes. Expectations that by the spring of 1862 a quick and easy victory would have been won were supplanted by prospects of a long and hard conflict. The effect of the changed outlook was greatly to depress the Southern spirit.

Another factor in the morale crisis of 1862 was a declining confidence of the people in their leaders. On

February 25, 1862, A. B. Bacon wrote to his friend President Davis: "I find our whole community in Louisiana and Mississippi . . . to have utterly lost their confidence in the generalship of Gen. A. S. Johnston." Joseph E. Johnston was severely criticized for his defensive tactics. On May 17, 1862, after that leader's withdrawal from the Williamsburg area, Robert Toombs wrote to Alexander H. Stephens: "McClellan was there with his whole army, a good deal less I think than ours, and we could have whipped as easily there as anywhere else. But as usual we burnt up everything and fled, were attacked in the retreat, and left in the hands of the enemy some ten or twelve hundred of our killed wounded and sick, and that *after a decided victory*. That is called generalship!!"

Polk, Lee, Beauregard and other generals likewise came in for some adverse comment in the early months of 1862. But most of the complaint was directed at the Confederate political leaders. An Alabamian, chafing under recent defeats, wrote on February 25, 1862: "I am almost on the verge of madness. . . . So far the people have done everything, the Government little, and this little in the wrong direction."

Congress and the cabinet were denounced as incompetent by some. Secretary of the Navy Mallory and Secretary of War Benjamin were objects of special attack. But it was Davis who bore the brunt of blame and who suffered the greatest loss of prestige. The chorus of acclaim which greeted his every move during the first months of the Confederacy had changed a year later into an ominous rumble of complaint and disparagement.

One of the main charges against the President was lack of aggressiveness in the conduct of the war. On

January 8, 1862, John M. Daniel of the Richmond *Examiner* in one of his first open criticisms of the administration stated: "The policy of monotonous defense which has been perseveringly pursued by the authorities of the Confederacy has been the subject of universal regret among the Southern people, of annoyance to our generals and of disease and death to our armies." Six weeks later he wrote: "The Yankees have outwitted us . . . they have managed their power with much more judgement; and that on just the point where the South was supposedly superior to the North—that is to say in the art of government—the Yankees have beaten us."

Daniel kept sniping at the administration during March and April and on May 19, 1862, he again focused his sights squarely on Davis. "The President proclaimed last Friday to be a day of official prayer and religious ceremony," he stated, and "the Departments were closed and the necessary work of this trying period was brought to a standstill for twenty-four hours." "These devotional proclamations of Mr. Davis have lost all good effect from their repetition," he added, and "are regarded by the people as either cant or evidences of mental weakness. . . . When we find the President standing in a corner telling his beads, and relying on a miracle to save the country, instead of mounting his horse and putting forth every power of the Government to defeat the enemy, the effect is depressing in the extreme. When the ship springs a leak, the efficient captain does not order all hands to prayers, but to the pumps. The same newspapers that are burdened with the news of the evacuation of Norfolk announce that President Davis had just been confirmed in the Episcopal Church."

Daniel was of course an exceptionally bitter critic of Davis, but his statements cannot be dismissed as the mere ranting of an extremist. Comments of many other prominent Southerners indicate a widespread dissatisfaction with the chief executive on the score of his Fabian policies. L. Q. Washington, one of Davis's aides, wrote to Mary Boykin Chesnut, May 2, 1862: "There is general discontent at the defensive policy which is pursued. It is thought by the best men that the policy is ruinous to the State and the cause and the feeling of hostility to it is intense. . . . All the blame falls on . . . [the President]. He is saddled with the whole responsibility by the public for the failure to advance on the enemy."

The President also was criticized for dispersing the Confederate forces, for trying to defend too many points instead of concentrating troops at a place of attack of the South's own choosing. He was condemned for surrounding himself with inferior advisers whom he could easily bend to his own will, attempting to browbeat Congress and impinging on the rights of the states. Some of his critics charged him with trying to establish a military despotism.

As evidence of an inclination toward tyranny these critics cited the President's request for authority to suspend the writ of habeas corpus, a request which Congress granted on February 27, 1862. This act, rushed through Congress in secret session with little debate, gave Davis the power to suspend the writ in cities, towns and military districts that he deemed in such danger of attack as to warrant declaration of martial law. Accordingly, Davis immediately proclaimed martial law in Norfolk and Portsmouth; and Richmond and Petersburg were placed under military rule early in March. Later, under the initial law or modified versions of it, martial law was applied to other localities.

Davis exercised with restraint and caution the power conferred upon him by the habeas corpus acts. But the same cannot be said of some of the local commanders who, without consulting the President, or by perversion of authority granted by him, initiated systems of military law that were unjustifiably oppressive. Under the best of conditions, military rule did not sit well with the people. Blame for the odious system centered on Davis and contributed greatly to the undermining of his prestige.

On April 16, 1862, a few weeks after authorizing the suspension of the habeas corpus writ, Congress enacted the first conscription act. This law, which declared every able-bodied male from 18 to 35 subject to Confederate military service, was passed at the suggestion of Lee and Joseph E. Johnston. But it was regarded as an "administration measure," and Davis was destined to bear the onus of its unpopularity.

The adverse effect of conscription on the morale of some of the plain people is evidenced by soldier letters written in the spring of 1862. A Virginia private of Hampton's Legion wrote his father on April 13, 1862: "The conscription bill now before Congress has been greatly under discussion of late. Its principal feature . . . immediate conscription by the associate government, in lieu of a requisition upon each State for all her arms-bearing citizens, militates so strongly against the sovereignty of the State and is so gross an usurpation of authority that I should be greatly shocked to see it pass unchallenged by my State. Such a surrender of the right for which above all others we are now contending would go far to make me renounce my allegiance to the State and wander into exile. . . . I trust, however, that before this infamy is consummated, the sky will grow so bright as to relieve the wretched triflers in Richmond from the panic which dictates such unconstitutional measures."

A Tar Heel private whose hopes of early release from service were blasted by the conscription act wrote two days after its passage: "My contemplated visit to N[orth] Carolina . . . is now amongst the 'hopes that are fled' & instead of that I am made a Soldier for ten years in all probability. . . . I would like to know what has been done with the main principal for which we are now fighting—*States Rights!*—Where is it? If such a measure was necessary to make our men enter or continue to fight for the cause we have in hand, then I think we are indeed in a bad fix. . . . I think the bill will prove very unpopular with the army. When we hear men comparing the despotism of the *Confederacy* with that of the Lincoln government—*something must be wrong.*"

A South Carolinian serving in Virginia on April 18, 1862, wrote his homefolk: "This Conscript Act will do away with all the patriotism we have. Whenever men are forced to fight they take no personal interest in it. . . . My private opinion is that our Confederacy is gone up or will go soon. . . . A more oppressive law was never enacted in the most uncivilized country or by the worst of despots. Remember what I say it will eventually be our ruin. . . . I am mad at the action of Congress and Jeff Davis and won't deny it."

Resentment of conscription was stronger among civilians than in the army. Some of the soldier wives who had just passed through a winter of loneliness and deprivation, and whose chief source of comfort was the prospect of an early return of their husbands, were cast into the depths of gloom by the law. Instead of enjoying the bliss of a reunited household, they were now forced to assume the responsibility of cultivating crops and supporting themselves and their children. To these burdens was added a gnawing concern for the safety of spouses now confronted with another season of fighting.

Disaffection created by the conscription act among the masses was nourished by the attitude of some of the leaders. Governor Brown of Georgia, Senator Orr of South Carolina, Senator Oldham of Texas, General Robert Toombs and Chief Justice R. M. Pearson of North Carolina all regarded the law as an unnecessary and unjustifiable encroachment on states' rights. One of the bitterest critics of the act was Vice-President Stephens who from the self-imposed exile of his home in Crawfordville, Georgia, in the summer of 1862 began to challenge various aspects of Davis's program. Conscription he denounced as "very bad policy." "We should have called for volunteers for the war, and no doubt they would have come," he stated. "It would have been better to rely upon soldiers thus recruited." Herschel V. Johnson, W. L. Yancey, Howell Cobb and other prominent leaders also were opposed to the Confederate draft law. Viewing the situation in the perspective of time the wisdom of the government in resorting to conscription seems questionable. Having made states' rights the basis of secession and a part of its organic law, the Confederacy was hard put to justify a course which so palpably violated the principle. To be effective conscription had to have the support of the state authorities and the masses of the people. This it never had, and the controversy and strife that it engendered did incalculable harm to public morale and the Confederate cause.

The total effect of military reverses, hard times and diminution of confidence in leadership was so depressing that even so prominent and convinced a Southerner as Herschel V. Johnson before the war's second winter despaired of Confederate success. In a remarkable letter written in confidence to a friend on October 25, 1862, Johnson stated: "You ask me if I have confidence in the success of the Southern Confederacy? I pray for success but I do not expect success. . . . The enemy in due time will penetrate the heart of the Confederacy. . . . and the hearts of our people will quake & their spirits will yield to the force of overpowering numbers. . . . The enemy is superior to us in everything but courage & therefore it is quite certain if war is to go on, until exhaustion overtake the one side or the other side, that we shall be the first to be exhausted."

Though Johnson loyally supported the Davis program throughout his subsequent career in the Confederate Senate there is nothing in his writing or his record to indicate that he ever changed the view of ultimate Southern defeat that he secretly registered during the second year of conflict.

In the summer of 1862 the country as a whole experienced a revival of spirit and this resurgence of optimism which extended into the fall marked the end of the Confederacy's first great morale crisis.

The upturn in public sentiment was due to several influences. The summer months brought increased activity both at home and in the army, and as soldiers became absorbed in marching and fighting and civilians in cultivating crops, attending revivals, picnics and barbecues, and participating in the countless other doings that were normal to the season, they shook off their megrims and became more hopeful. Curtailment of cotton and tobacco and concentration on food crops brought an improvement of diet. Inflation stimulated business. Warm weather reduced clothing needs and took restless children into the out-of-doors and thus brought some relief to harassed mothers.

More important than all of these in its effect on morale was the decided improvement in the military situation. In the east, after repelling Federal efforts to take Richmond, the Army of Northern Virginia under the brilliant leadership of Lee and Jackson won a tremendous victory at Manassas on August 29-30, and in September invaded Maryland. In the west the offensive launched by Grant at the beginning of the year bogged down with the coming of summer and in the autumn Confederate forces under Bragg and Kirby Smith marched deep into Kentucky. These spectacular achievements, accompanied as they were by favorable developments on the diplomatic front, brought Confederate fortunes to the highest point of the war and infused the Southern people with new hope and determination.

But morale did not approach the dizzy heights of the war's first months, and the revival that had swelled up in the summer and autumn began to lose its force with the coming of winter. The trend continued downward through the early months of 1863 despite manifestations of unprecedented discouragement among Northerners, and in the summer of 1863 the Confederacy entered its second great morale crisis.

* * * * *

The causes of the second crisis included those which produced the first, but there was some difference in their relative influence. Hardship played a greater part in depressing morale in 1863 than in 1862 because suffering was more intense and widespread, and the people were so ground down by war-weariness that many lacked the spiritual stamina to rise above their woes. Mounting prices, difficulties of transportation, hoarding, inadequacy of wages, tardiness of the government in meeting its financial obligations, lack of effective relief programs and failure of draft policies to provide exemption on the basis of dependents all combined to produce a vast amount of destitution in Southern homes and camps in 1863. Suffering was especially acute and prevalent among the poor non-slaveholding families of the hill and mountain sections and among the laborers of towns and cities. But many members of more privileged groups also felt the pinch of hardship during this period. Middle and upper class people who experienced the greatest hardship were white collar workers in urban communities, planter and professional families residing in invaded areas and refugees who fled from their homes to avoid living under Federal rule. The crowding of exiles into communities whose facilities were already overtaxed by the strains of war created problems for both natives and newcomers and often led to friction between them.

Refugees and others who were forced to leave their homes by the fortunes of war often moved in with relatives. In the Civil War as in the emergencies of our own time this doubling up with kinfolk frequently resulted in unhappiness for all concerned. Some of the most plaintive letters of the Confederate period are those of wives to their soldier husbands complaining of irritations and annoyances of living under the same roof with uncongenial in-laws.

The conviction that greedy and unprincipled schemers were shirking their responsibilities and using the war to advance their fortunes also did much to undermine public morale in 1863. The lowly people who provided the bulk of the Confederacy's fighting forces were especially susceptible to the belief that more privileged neighbors were taking unfair advantage of them. In some instances discontent among the women became so great that they indulged in rioting and pillage.

Dissatisfaction with leadership also contributed to the second morale crisis as it had to the first. But in 1863 discontent was focused more sharply than before on the Confederate government. Some of the military leaders were denounced but in general they received less censure for their failings than did the administration for entrusting them with high command.

One of the principal complaints against the government was that it favored the rich over the poor. The laws permitting the hiring of substitutes and exempting owners of twenty or more slaves were cited as examples of discrimination and increasing numbers of the lowly folk referred to the conflict as "a rich man's war and a poor man's fight."

Poor and rich alike found fault with the government on the score of its impressment and taxation policies. Southerners were unaccustomed to heavy taxation, and the descent upon them in 1863 of hordes of inquisitorial agents representing a distant government, demanding food, livestock and vehicles for little price or none at all, was, to say the least, exceedingly annoying. These visitations were made the more unpalatable by all-too-common instances of untactfulness, high-handedness and corruption on the part of the agents, and their tendency to concentrate on easily accessible areas. An added cause of dissatisfaction was the frequency with which produce gathered by these agents was permitted to rot in depots before the eyes of hungry civilians.

The impressment and tax programs and the manner in which they were administered diffused in the public mind the impression that the Confederate government was despotic and arbitrary and incapable of efficiently managing the affairs of the country. This idea was nurtured by other practices and tendencies observable by the people in 1863. One of these was the continuation in high position of officials who appeared incompetent, such as Bragg, Holmes, Northrop and Pemberton. Another was the breakdown of discipline in many military organizations and especially in commands far removed from the main centers of conflict. Members of these loosely controlled units roamed the countryside plundering the premises of helpless women whose husbands were on the fighting front, abusing them, taking away their provisions and livestock and threatening their very existence. Protests against these depredations usually were futile.

Dissatisfaction with the government and its policies was attested in congressional elections held in the fall of 1863. Many original secessionists who had vigorously supported the administration program, such as C. C.

Clay and J. L. M. Curry of Alabama, were replaced by men of Whig or Unionist background who had been lukewarm toward secession if not openly opposed to it, and who had been critical of the administration's policies.

The factor of greatest weight in the second morale crisis was defeat on the battle fronts. General Nathanial P. Banks' march through the Teche country of Louisiana in April and May produced great alarm in the Southwest. Early in July Lee was defeated at Gettysburg and Pemberton surrendered an army of 30,000 men at Vicksburg. The effect on public morale of these two disasters was tremendous. In their wake a cloud of gloom such as the Confederacy had never known settled over the land and the Southern spirit suffered an injury from which it never recovered.

The crushing depression was registered in scores of letters and diaries, by all classes of society and in all parts of the country. On July 11, 1863, a paroled private wrote his wife from Vicksburg: "I see no prospect now of the South ever sustaining itself. We have Lost the Mississippi and our nation is Divided and they is not a nuf left to fight for. I don't Look for eny thing Else but total anahighlation . . . of the South if She continue to carry on the war for we have a Powerfull nation fighting against us. they have Every thing . . . while we are half fed." On July 15, 1863, General Wade Hampton wrote Senator Wigfall: "We could better have stormed the Heights of Stafford than these at Gettysburg. I am thoroughly disgusted & nothing but a sense of duty would take me back to my unpleasant position." A Virginia private who was in the Gettysburg fight wrote afterward to his sister: "We got a bad whiping. . . . they are awhiping us . . . at every point . . . I hope they would make peace so that we that is alive yet would get home agane . . . but I supose Jef Davis and lee dont care if all is kiled."

On July 20 a lowly North Carolina woman wrote her soldier husband: "The people is all turning to Union here since the Yankees has got Vicksburg. I want you to come home as soon as you can after you git this letter." About the same time a Louisiana private stationed near Jackson, Mississippi, noted in his diary: "The men are low spirited and have been ever since they heard of the fall of Vicksburg. I never saw such depression." His observations were confirmed by a splendid Mississippi soldier of the same army who wrote his homefolk on July 19: "I have never felt like we were whiped until now."

On August 2, 1863, Robert G. H. Kean of the Confederate War Department stated in his diary: "People on the street corners are talking very much as if they thought we had about enough of this war." Four days later, Hugh Lawson Clay, another Richmond official, wrote his brother, Senator C. C. Clay: "The signs are portentious of calamity. In whatever quarter and to whatever department of the Government you look, there is nothing to cheer, to inspire hope. . . . Defeat and disaster come from every quarter . . . In Fine, all things seem working to our utter ruin. . . . Unless something is done to reassure the country and inspire us with new and better patriotism we are irretrievably gone."

The enormous despondency produced by Vicksburg and Gettysburg manifested itself in an epidemic of desertion and absence without leave. Officers' reports for July and August tell of men heading home by the scores, and at the end of July the Assistant Secretary of War estimated total absentees as 50,000 to 100,000.

Many of the absentees returned to their commands after a brief sojourn at home, but others, and probably a majority, contrived to avoid further service. A Georgian wrote his brother early in September 1863: "I have had my furlough extended twice and I expect to have it extended a third time if I can. if not I think I will Stay at home any how for my health is verry bad and there is no use of fighting any longer no how for we are done gon up the Spout the Confederacy is done whiped. . . . the Soldiers that went from this country that is alive is nearly all at home."

This soldier stated that staying at home presented no difficulty as the people were "nearly all unanimously against war holding any longer." As poor as morale became in the army during this period, it was better there than among civilians. Instances of men on the fighting front writing encouraging letters home appear to have been considerably more numerous than inspiriting letters flowing in the opposite direction.

The effects of Gettysburg and Vicksburg were especially depressing to people of the Trans-Mississippi country. A broadside was issued in Dallas County, Texas, in September, 1863, bearing the title "Common Sense," and signed "one who was at VICKSBURG." This sheet, the sentiments of which were the opposite of those expressed by Thomas Paine in his Revolutionary pamphlet of the same caption, told the people that they had been deluded by their leaders and pled with them to take affairs into their own hands and call a peace convention.

About the same time this broadside was issued Kirby

Smith, Commanding General of the Trans-Mississippi Department, wrote a gloomy letter to one of his principal subordinates in which he referred to the citizens of his department as "a lukewarm people, the touchstone to whose patriotism seems beyond my grasp, and who appear more intent upon the means of evading the enemy and saving their property than of defending their firesides."

Efforts for a peace convention did not get beyond the discussion stage, and Kirby Smith's military organization did not disintegrate. But the Trans-Mississippi fighting forces dwindled in size, discipline and combat efficiency and the zeal of the people languished. Texans, Louisianans and other western soldiers continued to display much gallantry under Lee, Bragg, Johnston and Hood and to show their mettle in defending their own country against Banks in the Red River Campaign. Many Trans-Mississippi civilians likewise loyally sustained the Confederacy to the end. But apathy and defection were far more prevalent than active patriotism. Indeed, it hardly seems extreme to state that after Vicksburg and Gettysburg the Trans-Mississippi, except for the service of its soldiers east of the river, played only a nominal role in the stand for Southern independence.

In the South as a whole public morale continued at very low ebb throughout the remainder of 1863 and the early months of 1864. During this period no decisive victories brightened the military horizon. Bragg failed to follow through at Chickamauga, and the walloping defeat of his army at Missionary Ridge, on November 25, 1863, culminating in the first mass panic of Johnny Rebs, deepened the gloom that already hung over the country. Prices continued to soar despite efforts of the treasury and

Congress to stabilize the currency. On January 1, 1864, a soldier stationed at Dalton, Georgia, wrote in his diary: "About the cheapest article a going now is Confederate blue backs they sell at five dollars a hundred with a fair prospect of falling as Congress has taken it in hand I suppose to try to better it but every thing they do appears to work the reverse way from what they intended."

Unabating hardship continued to weigh heavily on the public spirit and two measures enacted by the first Congress before it adjourned on February 17, 1864, aroused new fears of military despotism. One of these extended conscription to seventeen year-olds and men from forty-five to fifty and the other suspended the writ of habeas corpus throughout the South in cases of treason, desertion and sabotage. These acts were bitterly opposed by state authorities and resistance to them was so great in North Carolina and Georgia as virtually to nullify enforcement.

Some of the opposition in these states and elsewhere was inspired by demagogues and frustrated politicians who held deep grudges against President Davis. But beneath the dust clouds of their noisy protest lay a hard bed of genuine apprehension about local rights and individual liberties. In December, 1863, before the new laws were enacted, Jacob Thompson wrote Brigadier General J. R. Chalmers from Oxford, Mississippi, that the widespread discontent in his community "does not proceed from any disloyalty to our cause, or any unwillingness to make sacrifices . . . but it does arise . . . from what is regarded by the people as the unreasonable oppression of the Confederate authorities. . . . [who] burn their cotton, seize and confiscate their wagons . . . and subject themselves to great indignities." Three weeks later four constituents of Senator-elect James A. Graham wrote him from Salem, North Carolina: "Our people in this section of this State . . . feel outraged and indignant at the tyrannical & oppressive measures which the Executive & Congress have imposed & are imposing on a once free & happy people, the inevitable tendency of which (& we fear the design of many) is to overthrow every principle of State sovereignty & civil liberty, and the establishment of a military despotism with a Dictator at its head."

On February 22, 1864, shortly after passage of the new conscription and habeas corpus laws, August S. Merrimon wrote Senator Graham from Asheville, North Carolina: "The people are really alarmed, greatly alarmed, for the safety of our liberties under our forms of government."

Expressions such as these had considerable influence on state governors, legislators and Confederate Congressmen who as a rule were closer to the people and more familiar with public attitudes than were Davis and the cabinet. Graham, Oldham, Herschel Johnson, Vance, Milton and many others who opposed extension of conscription and renewal of habeas corpus suspension were well-meaning, patriotic men who sincerely thought that these acts would do more harm than good.

Early in 1864 a prominent Missourian, who wrote from Richmond that denunciation of the administration was more outspoken than ever before and that "the crisis of the war is upon us," added the statement that "a good currency law and a successful spring campaign will set everything right." The currency law, enacted on February 17, 1864, could hardly have been called a good one, but the spring campaign brought a measure of success. Banks was thwarted in his Red River expedition, Sherman's drive toward Atlanta was slowed down to a crawl by the skillful defensive tactics of Joseph E. Johnston and Grant's highly touted move against Richmond after terrible losses was side-tracked to Petersburg where it bogged down in a siege. These accomplishments on the fighting fronts, along with evidences of increasing peace sentiment in the North and prospects of good crops in the Confederacy, lifted the Southern spirit from the deep despondency that had enthralled it since Gettysburg and Vicksburg. Hence the second great morale crisis may be said to have ended about June, 1864. Morale did not recover to as great extent as it had in the previous revival, though public sentiment continued in a relatively healthy state throughout the summer and early fall.

In November the Southern spirit slumped again and in the winter of 1864-1865 the Confederacy experienced its third major morale crisis. From this crisis there was to be no recovery. * * * * *

The final crisis was precipitated by the reelection of Lincoln. For the return of Lincoln to the White House was interpreted as a defeat of the Union peace movement and an unmistakable sign of the North's determination to push the war to a successful conclusion. Even before the results of the balloting were known, a Mississippian informed President Davis of many soldiers writing home that if Lincoln was reelected they would desert as they could not endure the prospect of fighting for four more years. In February, 1865, a Floridian wrote a friend: "There is considerable desertion among the Fla. soldiers from Hood's and Lee's armys they say that both armys are greatly dispirited and have no hope of achieving our independence since the reelection of Lincoln." He added that "the general impression in this part of the Country is that we will be subjugated in a short time and many would be glad to have peace on almost any terms."

Discontent with the Confederate government reached unprecedented heights in the last winter of the conflict and contributed much to the final morale crisis. The administration was roundly denounced for its failure to stay the tide of inflation, feed the armies, and protect the citizenry from marauding of soldiers and abuses of the impressing agents, tax collectors and conscription officers who swarmed through the land.

Reverses on the fighting front also played an important part in the final crisis in Confederate morale. The complete failure of Price in Missouri, Hood's disastrous expedition into Middle Tennessee and Sherman's triumphant march through Georgia and South Carolina convinced many whose spirits had survived all prior misfortunes that further resistance was utterly useless.

The last winter of the war brought to Southern homes and camps greater suffering and misery than they had ever known before, and the burden was more than many could bear.

The collapse of the Southern spirit that marked the closing months of the war manifested itself in many ways. On the home front some of the most obvious signs were an almost complete breakdown of law and order, wholesale traffic with the Federals, an enormous deterioration of morals, flagrant defiance of conscription, an epidemic of hoarding and speculation and an unprecedentedly violent denunciation of President Davis. In the army fraternization with the men in blue reached alarming proportions, and desertion became so frequent that the fighting forces seemed on the verge of melting away.

In a ten-day period in March, 1865, Lee reported 1,094 desertions from his already depleted army; in one instance a brigade deserted *en masse*. On March 8, 1865, a North Carolina captain wrote his mother from Petersburg: "There have been a great many desertions lately but my company had never had one since the war commenced until one night last week when four of my men deserted." "Most of the desertions, lately," he added, "have been caused by letters from home."

Demoralization at home and in the army was vividly reflected in a letter written by Hugh Lawson Clay, from Richmond, February 15, 1865. "I see nothing but defeat, disaster & ruin to result from the present conduct of affairs," he stated. "Congress and the Executive are antagonized upon matters of little moment. . . . Our army has been dwindling until neither one is large enough to withstand an attack in [the] open field. There is collapse in Every Department—and more than that there is an utter loss of confidence by the people in the Administration, in Congress, and in the success of the cause itself."

The will to win had become so feeble by the close of the war's last winter that any expectation of again reviving it to a point of effective resistance was wishful thinking of the extremest sort. Hence the final battles about Richmond and in the West were but tragic afterglows of a fire that had already died.

The fire had burned brightest in the months that followed Fort Sumter, and its blaze was then so dazzling as to conceal from view the splinters of dissidence that lay in the background. In the winter of 1861-1862, the flames subsided perceptibly under the dampening effects of the first military reverses, disillusionment with high leadership and the dawning prospect of a long, hard conflict. Spectacular achievements by the armed forces and favorable developments at home rekindled the fire in the autumn of 1862, though not to its initial brilliance. The enormous setbacks at Gettysburg and Vicksburg, followed by increasing hardship and further decline of leader prestige reduced the flame to such low intensity that it seemed in danger of dying, and it continued to burn very weakly until the summer of 1864. Evidences of disaffection in the North and a hopeful turn of military events quickened the fire for a time in the summer of 1864, but the reelection of Lincoln, a series of disasters on the battlefield, deepening discontent with the government and an unprecedented burden of hardship and war-weariness brought a flood of despair in the fall and winter of 1864-1865 which reduced the fire to smouldering coals and finally quenched it altogether.

Total extinguishment of course, is a figure applicable only to the collective spirit of the country. For the Confederacy contained many individuals whose will to win remained undaunted from the beginning to the end of the conflict. The army had a lion's share of staunch spirits, of men who marched without murmur in their bare feet and fought valiantly against tremendous odds on empty stomachs in battle after battle. They were inured to hardship, they believed in the rightness of their cause and they had a fierce pride in themselves, their units, their leaders and their bullet-riddled colors. Typical of these gray-clad heroes who remained firm amid a sea of defection was a lowly private who when the surrender was announced at Appomattox stepped up to his commander, grasped him by the hand and sobbed: "Goodby, General; God bless you, we will go home, make three more crops, and try them again."

While morale of the army was always better than that of civilians, the homefront was by no means devoid of unwavering spirits. Among the civilian stalwarts was a colorful and eccentric old Texan named Gideon Lincecum. Though he often railed out against the bungling of leaders, his will to win survived every Confederate disaster. Shortly after the fall of Fort Henry and Fort Donelson he wrote: "We have among us, it is true, a good many dead heads, besides real enemies and some neutral. But let us move onwards with the irresistable tramp of stern resolves; we cannot be conquered." The loss of Vicksburg he took in stride, and even argued that it would redound to the good of the Confederate cause.

An important influence in maintaining Lincecum's spirit was a deep and insatiable hatred of Yankees. On July 27, 1863, he wrote: "There is nothing right or honorable in that villianous people. They are begot, bred and borne by . . . their fanatic priests; raised & trained by disappointed and badly soured old maids. . . . And it would be a great piece of weakness in our government to listen to any overtures . . . for a suspension of hostilities at any time, even to bury their dead. They care nothing for the dead, nor further than their expectation of gain goes, for the living. They be damned."

On March 9, 1865, as the mantle of defeat was settling over the Confederacy, he wrote hopefully of the coming campaigns. "I have never felt any uneasiness in respect to the finale of this revolution," he stated. "Success . . . is certain sooner or later, and now I feel doubly assured." A letter of April 27, 1865, expressed enthusiastic approval of Lincoln's assassination. "I hope the man who performed that great piece of public service to the nation," he stated, "may make good his escape, and that he may live to burst the souls of a few more of the despots." "As to the fate of Lee's army," he added, "we may, to be sure look upon it as one amongst our disasters, but we must mend it by renewed energy, and at last, if we cannot force the envading robbers from our soil, we can all die in the effort."

Unwavering spirits were to be found among all classes of Southern society. But the record of the plain people seems to be better than that of the more privileged groups. As already indicated defection among them was widespread, and especially so during the last two years of the war. But their hardship was much greater than that of their better situated neighbors and they had less at stake than the owners of slaves. No one was called on to endure as great privation as the wives of yeomen and laborers whose husbands were in the army and who had to sustain large families in the midst of ever increasing inflation and scarcity. Yet in the last months of the war, when planters turned deaf ears to the urgent calls of Lee for slaves to strengthen his fortifications, and when throughout the land people of means hoarded their abundance in anticipation of higher prices, many of these noble women remained firm in their devotion to the Southern cause and in barely literate letters urged their soldier husbands to do their full duty.

Chapter 3 FAILURES THAT WERE FATAL

IN THE YEARS since Appomattox millions of Southerners have attributed Confederate defeat to the North's overpowering strength. This is a comforting conclusion and it is not without a substantial basis of fact. For the North unquestionably had an immense superiority of material and human resources. But the North also faced a greater task. In order to win the war the North had to subdue a vast country of nine million inhabitants, while the South could prevail by maintaining a successful resistance. To put it another way, the North had to conquer the South while the South could win by outlasting its adversary, by convincing the North that coercion was impossible or not worth the effort. The South had reason to believe that it could achieve independence. That it did not was due as much, if not more, to its own failings as to the superior strength of the foe. What were some of the internal influences that shackled the South's effort and contributed to its defeat?

Perhaps the most costly of the Confederacy's short-comings was the disharmony among its people. A cursory glance at the Confederacy reveals numerous instances of bitter strife, and one who delves deeply into the literature of the period may easily conclude that Southerners hated each other more than they did the Yankees. Behind the battle of bullets waged with the invaders was an enormous war of words and emotions among Confederates themselves which began before secession and which eventually became so intense that it sapped the South's vitality and hastened Northern victory.

One of the most notorious instances of disharmony was that of the President and Vice-President. Davis and Stephens got along amicably in the early days of the Confederacy but differences in political background and the fact that both were sickly, stubborn and sensitive, worked against continuing cordiality. Stephens chafed under the inactivity inherent in his position and when Davis in the autumn of 1861 ceased turning frequently to him for counsel a coolness developed between them. Using ill health as an excuse, Stephens in 1862 spent about half of his time in Georgia. Before the end of 1862 he was denouncing conscription and other major acts of the administrative program. In 1863 he virtually abandoned the vice-presidency and launched an open attack on Davis and his policies. His antagonism increased with the passing of time and in 1864 he teamed up with his brother, Linton Stephens, and Governor Joseph E. Brown of Georgia in an all-out effort to discredit Davis and his conduct of the government and initiate steps looking to peace and reunion. In March, 1864, the Confederacy was treated to the spectacle of its Vice-President castigating the President and the administration in a three hour speech before the Georgia Legislature.

Principle entered to some extent into the disagreement between Davis and Stephens, as the Vice-President insisted that the sovereignty of the state should always be preeminent while Davis believed that at least during the war both states and individuals should yield to the central government some of their accustomed rights. But Professor James Z. Rabun, who has made a careful study of the war-time relations of Stephens and Davis, attributes their quarrel primarily to pettiness, jealousy and blindness on the part of the Vice-President. It is possible that Davis could have prevented the break by playing to Stephens's vanity and making him a more active partner in the administration, but flattery was not among the President's talents. And Stephens could never have been enthusiastic about a secondary role. The Vice-President's course would have been more admirable if he had resigned in 1862. For him to stay in the administration and openly fight it was as unbecoming to the man as it was hurtful to the Southern cause.

Relations between Davis and his cabinet appeared relatively harmonious, but beneath the smooth surface considerable tension existed. Significant of the smouldering dissatisfaction was the fact that Davis made eight changes in a cabinet of six members, and four of these were in the war office. In contrast, Lincoln made only five changes in his official family of seven members. Only two of Davis's cabinet members, Mallory and Reagan, held their posts throughout the war, and if Davis had known what Mallory was writing in his diary about the conduct of the government he would probably have given the navy another head before the war was a year old.

Benjamin was the only cabinet member with whom Davis maintained a warm and close relationship, and the cordiality was due in no small part to Benjamin's adeptness at flattery. Most of the others chafed at the seeming unimportance of their positions and some resented the President's failure to take them more fully into his confidence. Randolph, as previously noted, left the cabinet in a huff, and Toombs and Hunter both became bitter opponents of Davis after their resignations.

Davis's difficulties with the cabinet were as nothing in comparison with the dissension between the President and the Congress. Cleavage between the executive and legislative branches first became noticeable in the summer of 1861. Initial disharmony was due in part to disagreement over appointments. Fire-eaters thought the President gave too many offices to anti-secessionists and anti-secessionists in turn accused him of showing partiality to the fire-eaters. Delegations from one state complained that their constituents were being neglected in favor of those of another. Some of the generals had admirers in Congress who were quick to denounce any mistreatment, fancied or real, of their military heroes. Beauregard had an especially strong following in Congress: Wigfall, Pryor and Chesnut served as voluntary aides to him in 1861, and in February, 1862, his brother-in-law, Charles J. Villere, entered Congress. When the President and the "Grand Creole" had their first disagreement in the autumn of 1861 over who was to blame for not following up the victory at Manassas, Beauregard's partisans in Congress jumped to his defense and heaped denunciation on the President's head. Some of them even accused the President of having gone to the battlefield on the day of the fight with a view of stealing the glory from Beauregard and Johnston.

Beauregard's correspondence indicates that he kept in close touch with his friends in Congress, and that he did not hesitate to seek their aid in time of need. In following this course he was by no means unique among Confederate generals. Even the pious Jackson asked the assistance of his Congressman, A. R. Boteler, on several occasions and once obtained Boteler's interposition in a quarrel with Secretary Benjamin.

The Mallory diary indicates that wives had a part in the initial estrangement of President and Congress. On June 12, 1861, the Navy Secretary noted: "At the [dining] table devoted to the Pres'd't & Cabinet & his company, Mr. [and] Mrs. Wigfall also sit; and Mrs. Wigfall evidently has determined to *snub* Mrs. Davis & her sister Miss Howel[l] Her manner is a perfect rebuke & her air one of toleration & suferance. But Mrs. D. and Miss H. are the last women to take such an exhibition quietly; & consequently there is a perpetual cross fire of sharpshooting in an amicable way. Cutting things are said blandly; and quiet smiles . . . cover rifle balls." On June 14 Mallory wrote: "More squabbles & covert sarcasm at table. Mrs. Wigfall evidently thinks that Mrs. Davis regrets her presence at table & she affects great indifference if not contempt from [for] all Mrs. Davis says." The entry for June 23 reports a truce between the feminine contestants, but the feud smouldered on and probably contributed to the rupture which occurred between Davis and Senator Wigfall a few months later and which eventually developed into one of the bitterest antagonisms known to the Confederacy. Other women were drawn into the controversy, including Mrs. Joseph E. Johnston, who was an intimate of the Wigfalls, and the Quartermaster General's wife, the beautiful Mrs. Myers, who, as previously stated, did her husband irreparable injury by calling Mrs. Davis an "old squaw." Varina Davis's situation was made the more difficult by the seclusion forced on her by the President's frail health, the jealousy which her position naturally aroused, and the inclination of the Virginia blue-bloods, with whom Mrs. Joseph E. Johnston associated, to despise the Western upbringing of the Confederacy's first lady.

Relations between Davis and Congress worsened considerably in the latter part of 1861, and by the following spring they had deteriorated to the point of open hostility on the part of many of the legislators. Several influences contributed to this heightening of antipathy, the most important of which was growing dissatisfaction with the President's conduct of the war. The series of defeats experienced by the South in the winter and spring were charged to Davis's addiction to dispersion and defense, and his reliance on incompetent advisors. His advocacy of conscription, impressment and the suspension of the writ of habeas corpus also alienated a goodly number of Congressmen, including some who in the interest of the common good cast their votes in favor of these measures.

The success of Davis in securing enactment of these and other administrative measures has tended to obscure the scope and intensity of the Congressional reaction against Davis that took place in 1862. Mrs. Davis in her memoir refers to the new Congress that assembled in February, 1862, as being less friendly to her husband than the group it superseded. She goes on to state: "Now for the first time there appeared to be an organized party in opposition to the Administration." This was putting the situation all too mildly. A piecing together of evidence gleaned from letters, diaries and other contemporary sources indicates that behind the scenes a strong and bitter attack was launched against the President in Congress, and that some who participated in it were determined to force Davis from office. On March 16, 1862, Thomas R. R. Cobb wrote his wife that Congress was secretly debating the deposition of Davis and added: *"He would be deposed* if the Congress had any more confidence in Stephens than in him."

The antagonists of Davis in Congress, realizing that prospects of getting rid of him were dim, set about to clip his wings. With a view of ousting the despised Benjamin and preventing the President's personal control of military operations they tried to secure the appointment of Lee as Secretary of War. Davis refused to make this change on the ground that the war office should be headed by a civilian. Congress then passed an act requiring the chief executive to appoint a commanding general who should have authority to take personal command of any field army at any time. Davis vetoed this measure on the ground that it violated his constitutional rights as commander-in-chief. At the same time he ordered Lee to Richmond and charged him under the President's direction with the conduct of the South's military operations. The President thus scored a victory over his Congressional enemies, for he used Lee in an advisory capacity only and continued to exercise as much control over operations as before. Congress did succeed in its efforts to force Benjamin from the war office, but this accomplishment was deprived of its appeasing effects when Davis on March 17, 1862, appointed Benjamin Secretary of State.

The President further antagonized Congress by his removal of Beauregard from command of the Army of Tennessee in June, 1862. As previously noted, fifty-nine of the legislators entered a written protest against the removal and the manner in which it was done. But when the protest was presented to the President by members of the Louisiana delegation he rejected it with a brusqueness that added fuel to the flame of congressional antipathy.

Even in its early stages the quarrel between Davis and Congress was marked by extreme bitterness. In May, 1862, L. M. Keitt, who had abandoned legislative halls for the battlefield but who maintained close contact with Richmond, wrote his wife: "it seems that things are coming to this pass; to be a patriot you must hate Davis." And some of Keitt's former colleagues freely voiced their hatred by denouncing Davis as an imbecile and a stubborn fool.

Tension between Chief Executive and Congress eased to some extent in the autumn of 1862, owing largely to the great improvement in the military outlook, but in the summer of 1863 relations again deteriorated and early in 1864 they reached another crisis.

A number of the new members who took their seats in the Congress that assembled in February, 1864, had been elected the preceding fall on anti-administration platforms. These newcomers joined old enemies of Davis in attributing recent military disasters to the President's incompetency and mismanagement. Friends of Beauregard took special pains to point up the fact that things would have been different if Davis had not unjustly removed their hero from command of the Army of Tennessee.

The President did not help his standing with Congress by making Bragg his chief military adviser and defying Congress by appointing Lawton Quartermaster General.

Intensification of Congressional antipathy to Davis early in 1864 led to a renewed effort to curb his power. Specifically, attempts were launched by Wigfall, Miles and others to require a change of cabinet with each new Congress and to divest the President of his control over the military forces. These proposals involved constitutional prerogatives and they did not get beyond the discussion stage.

Debates in Congress throughout 1864, over such touchy matters as the suspension of habeas corpus, impressment, finance and military policy, were marked by severe denunciation of the President. Davis had staunch friends in both House and Senate who defended him and his policies with great persistence and ability. But their efforts to promote concord between Davis and their colleagues were of little avail.

The year 1865 brought an increase of discord. In February Congress and the Virginia Legislature forced the resignation of Secretary Seddon and compelled Davis to make Lee general-in-chief of the armies. When the Congressmen adjourned on March 18, 1865, with the Union forces pressing in on the capital for the kill, they and the President were probably angrier with each other than at any prior period of the war.

* * * * *

Relations between Davis and his generals also left much to be desired. The most notable cases of disharmony were those of the President with Joseph E. Johnston and Beauregard. The first known rupture between the President and Johnston occurred in September, 1861. On August 31, 1861, Davis sent to the Senate the names of five officers for confirmation as full generals. Prior Confederate legislation had provided that the relative rank of these and other officers should be determined by their former commissions in the United States army. Johnston held the permanent rank of colonel in the old army, but when he became Quartermaster General in 1860 he was automatically promoted to brigadier general, as the new position called for that grade. Hence when Johnston resigned from the Federal service he was a brigadier general, and he was the only officer among those entering the Confederate army from the old service who held a general's rank at the time of resignation. He expected to be at the head of the list sent to the Senate on August 31, 1861. But Davis, according to an explanation made after the war, considered permanent rank as the only measure for determining seniority, and on that basis he listed the five nominees for general in this order: Samuel Cooper, Albert Sidney Johnston, Robert E. Lee, Joseph E. Johnston and P. G. T. Beauregard, and thus they were confirmed.

Davis later justified his action on the ground that the Quartermaster Generalcy was a staff position, carrying with it no right to command troops, and Johnston, had he remained in the Federal service, would have reverted to a colonelcy at the end of his staff tour. The applicable Confederate legislation, however, did not specify that generals were to be ranked by their line ratings, but simply stated that they would be rated according to their *commission* in the old army. Davis himself was responsible for the interpretation that made Johnston fourth instead of first among the Confederate generals. And he was inconsistent in the application of his formula, else Cooper, who had little line experience and whose promotions above captain had come in connection with staff positions, would have been given a lower rank. The top men, Cooper and Albert Sidney Johnston, were two of Davis's closest friends among the old army group.

When Joseph E. Johnston saw the listing of generals he was furious. He immediately wrote an 1800-word protest to the President; after holding it for two days to allow himself to cool off, he sent it forward without change. It was now Davis's turn to be angry, and his temper must have boiled as he read the general's scathing charges that he had disregarded both law and justice in denying Johnston first place among the generals. Thirty-nine words sufficed for the President's response; it was one of the shortest letters that he ever wrote, but it was also one of the coldest. Dated September 14, 1861, it read: "Sir—I have just received and read your letter of the 12th instant. Its language is, as you say, unusual; its arguments and statements utterly one sided, and its insinuations as unfounded as they are unbecoming. I am, &c—Jeff'n Davis."

Whatever their relations may have been before, there was no real harmony between Davis and Johnston after this angry flare-up of September, 1861. They were both proud and sensitive men, and they were honorable. But mutual trust, that essential ingredient of true concord, was gone from their relationship.

One has only to read their correspondence to sense the deep antagonism between them. In Johnston's view the authority of an army commander in time of war was virtually unlimited in the area of his jurisdiction. Hence he was annoyed by the President's seeming inclination to obtrude himself into the army's internal affairs. His extreme slowness in adopting Davis's insistent suggestion that regiments of the same state be brigaded together was doubtless due in part to a feeling that Davis was out of line in making such a proposal. And when Davis defended Benjamin in a quarrel that grew out of the Secretary's furloughing men and issuing orders to subordinate officers in the Army of Northern Virginia, Johnston was wrathful and understandably so.

Johnston's sensitiveness to prerogative and distrust of Davis, combined with a natural disposition to reticence, caused him to reveal very little of his activities and plans to the President, and this in turn was most annoying to Davis who often complained to the general and others that he was inadequately informed of Johnston's doings and intentions.

When Johnston recovered from his Seven Pines wound he desired more than anything else to return to his former command, or as he put it in a letter to Senator Wigfall "to be replaced where the Yankee missiles found me." Davis in assigning him instead to command of all the forces between the Appalachians and the Mississippi, including the armies of Bragg and Pemberton, insisted that he was giving him the highest military position in the Confederacy. But Johnston thought otherwise: Pemberton's and Bragg's forces were too far apart, he argued, to permit of effective command by one person; for an itinerant superior to take charge of them in succession would be impracticable and unfair both to the superior and to the army commander who was temporarily displaced. Johnston's letters to Wigfall reveal that he regarded the Western command not as an honor, but as a sort of glorified inspector generalship conferred by Davis to put him on the shelf. If Davis was sincere in his claim that the command was of prime importance, said Johnston, then he should give it to Lee, the Confederacy's first ranking field commander, and send him back to the Army of Northern Virginia. (Johnston's disappointment at not being returned to his old command on one occasion caused him to register a twinge of jealousy of Lee. On hearing of the Federal defeat at Fredericksburg he wrote Wigfall: "What luck some people have. Nobody will come to attack me in such a place.")

On January 3, 1863, after looking over his new command, Johnston restated to Davis his objections to the assignment and added: "With these views I earnestly beg some other position which may give me better opportunity to render such service as I may be capable of." But Davis refused to transfer him and in so doing helped to set the stage for Vicksburg.

It is interesting to speculate on what might have happened if Lee had been sent west in December, 1863, and Johnston returned to the command of the Army of Northern Virginia. Lee probably would not have deemed the direction of two armies as impracticable as did Johnston; his greater tact would have brought more effective cooperation with Richmond; and his decisiveness and boldness might have caused greater difficulty for Grant and Rosecrans. Johnston, while a brilliant tactician, especially in defensive operations, would hardly have won such victories as those of Second Manassas and Chancellorsville; but at the same time he might have avoided such a costly defeat as Gettysburg. It seems reasonable to think that Johnston would have been more effective in the East than he was in the West, and that Lee's aggressive methods were more vitally needed in Mississippi than in Virginia. In view of all the factors involved, it appears unlikely that Pemberton's army would have been lost had Lee and Johnston changed places in December, 1862. But the shift probably would not have changed the outcome of the war.

These are only speculations. The fact remains that Johnston stayed on in the West. Misunderstanding and discord with Davis increased and Vicksburg was lost. After Vicksburg the war of words between the two became more intense, and Johnston grew firmer in the opinion that Davis held a grudge against him, would never give him real support and would use him as a scapegoat for the failure of others. He was sustained in these views by members of the anti-Davis clique in Congress, and especially by Wigfall, with whom he held frequent correspondence and whose hatred of the President raged with increasing fury.

While Wigfall fed anti-Davis venom to Johnston, Benjamin pumped anti-Johnston poison into the President. According to Secretary Mallory, Benjamin delighted in directing at the President such remarks as these: "I have read much of obstinacy & perversity of commanding officers, but Johnston's pig-headedness excels anything I ever heard of."

"We'll never have a fight of his army as long as Johnston keeps at the head of it."

"Johnston is determined not to fight; it is of no use to reenforce him."

Johnston took over Bragg's army after Missionary Ridge, but he and Davis disagreed over the plan of campaign; and as the general's distrust of the President increased, he became ever more uncommunicative. In July the President sent Bragg to confer with Johnston but it seems likely that he had decided to put Hood in command before Bragg left the capital.

Congress and public opinion finally forced restoration of Johnston to command in February, 1865, but the change was made through the agency of Lee whom the President under pressure had appointed general-in-chief. Johnston and Davis were brought together briefly at Greensboro after Lee's surrender where in cold formality they exchanged opposing views as to future moves. But peace with the Yankees did not bring a similar blessing to the President and the general. They carried on their private war for the rest of their lives. In 1885, four years before he died, Davis stated in a letter to L. B. Northrop: "Joe Johnston I see is to have an office under the new Administration, so that rewards for treachery have not ceased with radical rule."

Davis and Beauregard seem to have been on cordial terms during the first months of the Confederacy. Relations were strained by a letter that Beauregard wrote on July 29, 1861, to two congressmen who had served as his voluntary aides, and which they read to their colleagues in secret session, charging the failure to march promptly on Washington after Manassas to shortcomings in the supply system. Davis was irked by this accusation. His reproof of the general was mild and Beauregard's response apologetic, but when Davis in late October read Beauregard's 9,000-word report of the battle (a digest of which was published in the Richmond *Dispatch* before the president even saw the document itself) he was more than annoyed. The report was highly self-laudatory and Davis interpreted it as an unjustifiable effort of Beauregard to blow up his own achievement. In a frostily formal letter Davis sharply rebuked the general for attempting "to exalt yourself at my expense" and took issue with some of the report's specific statements. He also began to call witnesses to sustain his position. Beauregard came back immediately with a long and vain statement bearing the dateline "Centreville, Virginia, withing hearing of the Enemy's Guns, November 3, 1861," which was addressed to the editors of the Richmond *Whig,* and published in that paper. The fight between Davis, the President, whose deepest yearning was for glory in battle, and the general, who considered himself a second Napoleon, was now openly joined.

Reference has already been made to the embittering effects of Davis's removal of Beauregard from his western command in June, 1862. Space will not permit a detailed tracing of subsequent developments in the controversy, but the quarrel raged with varying intensity throughout the war and was continued with the pen in the years that followed.

Other generals with whom Davis had misunderstandings or quarrels were D. H. Hill, M. L. Bonham and

Robert Toombs. Hill had been appointed lieutenant general in July, 1863, and assigned to the Army of Tennessee. After Chickamauga he joined fellow officers in asking for Bragg's removal on grounds of incompetency. But the President, on Bragg's recommendation, relieved Hill of his command and refused to submit his appointment as lieutenant general to the Senate for confirmation. Davis justified denial of the promotion on the ground that no corps was available for Hill to command. Hill attributed the action to spite for his opposition to Bragg, and pointed out that Lieutenant Generals Kirby Smith, Longstreet and Polk were not commanding corps but departments. He further stated that Major Generals Ransom and Whiting had recently been offered promotion. "It is hard to bear a life-time of humiliation," wrote the aggrieved Hill to his friend Senator J. A. Graham in 1864, "through the vindictiveness, unmerited and unprovoked, of [Davis] the most malignant man on earth."

While Hill was a West Pointer, Bonham and Toombs were civilian soldiers. Bonham had served as an officer in the Mexican War. He was appointed brigadier in the Confederate army in April, 1861, and participated in the first battle of Manassas. He incurred Davis's displeasure by protesting the President's relative ranking of generals who had served in the old army. He regarded himself the victim of personal pique and West Point prejudice when Davis promoted Beauregard and others over him and then deprived him of his command, on what Bonham termed a "miserable technicality which could have been avoided." "It is more than I can bear," he wrote Congressman Miles on December 7, 1861. In 1862, he resigned, went home and was elected governor of South Carolina.

When Toombs entered the army his relations with the President were by no means warm. Relations were not helped by Toombs's insubordinate conduct and his denunciation of the dilatory manner in which West Pointers were conducting the war. Disgust with what he regarded as persecution by the regular army group, including Davis, and failure to win promotion after conspicuous gallantry at Second Manassas and Antietam (in the former engagement he is said to have dashed up to his brigade waving his hat and shouted, "Go it boys, I am with you again. Jeff Davis can make a general but it takes God Almighty to make a soldier!") caused him to resign his commission and return to Georgia in 1863. There he gave full vent to his hatred of the President.

In the quarrels of Davis and his generals both sides were at fault. But this fact did not diminish the bitterness of these malignant controversies or lessen their injury to the Southern cause.

*   *   *   *   *

Even more damaging to the Confederacy was the disharmony between Davis and the governors. At one time or another the President came into conflict with most of the state executives, and the issue was usually some aspect of states' rights. These controversies, which were especially serious in the cases of Brown and Vance, have been ably treated by Professor Frank L. Owsley and others, and it is not necessary to review them here. When a government founded on the principle of states' rights became engaged in a war that taxed to the utmost every resource, considerable disagreement over national and state prerogative was to be expected. But these disagreements ought not to have degenerated into angry, irreconcilable quarrels between state and national executives, and the fact that they did reflects discreditably on all who were involved. He who in the relative calm of the present reads the correspondence of two honest, patriotic and well-meaning men like Davis and Vance cannot but be startled when he encounters a statement such as that contained in the President's letter of March 31, 1864, to the North Carolina governor. "There are other passages of your letter," Davis wrote, "in which you have so far infringed the proprieties of official intercourse as to preclude the possibility of reply. In order that I may not again be subjected to the necessity of making so unpleasant a remark, I must beg that a correspondence so unprofitable in its character and which was not initiated by me, may here end, and that your future communications be restrained to such matters as may require official action." It is not surprising that subsequent correspondence between the two executives was infrequent and formal.

Disharmony between Davis and some of the newspaper editors was characterized by similar acrimony. Presidential relations with Rhett of the Charleston *Mercury* and Daniel and Pollard of the Richmond *Examiner* were especially bitter. The attacks of these editors had a strongly personal flavor and were sometimes flagrantly insulting in their tone. After the fall of Vicksburg, Daniel wrote a violent editorial attributing the catastrophe to the President's blind and stubborn attachment to Pemberton. "Had the people dreamed that Mr. Davis would carry all his chronic antipathies, his bitter prejudices, his puerile partialities, and his doting favoritisms into the presidential chair," he stated, "they would never have allowed him to fill it."

* * * * *

The same type of discord that marred presidential relations was to be found in many other Confederate organizations and groups. There was much friction between Secretary of War Seddon and Adjutant General Cooper and between Seddon and Bragg after the latter became Davis's chief military adviser. Benjamin was thoroughly disliked by some, if not most, of his colleagues, in the cabinet. Congress sniped away periodically at the cabinet as a whole and launched major attacks on Benjamin, Mallory, Walker, Memminger and Seddon. The Confederate lawmakers also quarreled among themselves. H. S. Foote of Tennessee was the center of a vast amount of controversy. Late in the war, on the pretext of promoting peace, he abandoned the Confederacy and was expelled from the House of Representatives. While most of the conflict that raged in the legislative chambers was verbal, contests marked by physical violence were not unknown. During an angry debate in the Senate over the establishment of a Confederate supreme court, Benjamin H. Hill hurled an inkstand at William L. Yancey, and split the Alabamian's cheek. In the house, H. S. Foote provoked a fight with E. S. Dargan of Alabama by calling him a damned rascal. Dargan rushed at Foote with a bowie knife but was forcibly restrained by other members. As Dargan lay helplessly pinned to the floor by his colleagues, Foote struck a pose and exclaimed melodramatically: "I defy the steel of the assassin." During a committee session Foote exchanged blows with Thomas B.

Hanly of Arkansas and in an encounter at the Ballard House he was hit over the head with an umbrella by Congressman William G. Swan of Tennessee.

On August 31, 1861, John F. Henry, a Confederate officer stationed at Sikeston, Missouri, wrote his father, Gustavus A. Henry, who later became a Confederate Senator: "Somehow or other our officers here . . . don't work together. . . . Polk, Pillow and Cheatham . . . are all pulling in opposite directions." This young Tennesseean hit upon one of the great weaknesses of the Confederacy. Its generals, like its politicians, all too often pulled in opposite directions. Some of the discord among the military leaders had its origin in state sensitiveness and jealousy. Wade Hampton, for example, thought "Jeb" Stuart was partial to Virginia subordinates, and he deeply resented the alleged discrimination. Another glimpse of state jealousy is afforded by a letter of Bragg's chief of staff to Joseph E. Johnston after Chickamauga. "I tell you these Kentuckians understand getting along," he wrote; "the moment the battle is over Preston nominates his colonels for brigades; Buckner [recommends] Preston for the Division [command]; the corollary [is] that [Buckner] the [division] commander must be a Lieut. [General]." But a more common basis of disharmony was the strong belief among generals of civilian background that West Point officers functioned as a closed corporation in assignments and promotions. Toombs's difficulties with his superiors undoubtedly derived in part from his deep distrust of West Point graduates. Lack of confidence in soldierly abilities was another cause of dissension. Some quarrels among the generals seem to have had no other foundation than personal dislike.

In the Army of Northern Virginia some of the better known controversies were those of Jackson with A. P. Hill, Robert Toombs with D. H. Hill (Toombs challenged Hill to a duel for reproving him during the battle of Malvern Hill) and Longstreet with McLaws. The generous and tactful Lee set a splendid example of harmony though he seems to have fallen out with George E. Pickett in the closing days of the war.

The Western theaters were hotbeds of dissension. In the Trans-Mississippi, Price quarreled with McCulloch, Holmes had difficulty with Price and Taylor broke with Kirby Smith. But the principal center of discord in the whole Confederate army was the headquarters of Braxton Bragg. Strife between Bragg and his subordinates began on the Kentucky campaign of 1862, was intensified by the Murfreesboro campaign, and swelled to flood tide after Chickamauga. The angry charges and countercharges which passed between the army commander and his generals were echoed in the halls of Congress and in the councils of the President. Principals in the quarrel with Bragg were Leonidas Polk, J. C. Breckinridge, Simon B. Buckner, D. H. Hill and T. C. Hindman; but at one time or another many other generals were involved.

Governors and generals also squabbled. For example, Reynolds of Missouri was involved in an extremely bitter controversy with Price, and Watts of Alabama became so antagonistic to Bragg after the latter became Davis's military adviser that he refused to do business with him. Officials of the army and navy lashed at each other. Examples of discord that was nothing short of endemic could easily be multiplied. Strife was the Confederacy's evil genius and no major organization or activity escaped its crippling influence.

It would be easy to exaggerate the prevalence of dissension in the Confederacy, as quarreling tends to receive more notice in newspapers, diaries, memoirs and other sources on which the historian must lean, than does concord. Then, one must not forget that war creates unusual strains and therefore tends to enhance contention among any people. With due allowance for these considerations, I am convinced that Confederates were abnormally quarrelsome and that dissension was considerably more prevalent among them than among their opponents.

* * * * *

The assumption that Confederates were excessively contentious naturally raises the question: why? A number of reasons suggest themselves. One is the exaggerated individualism which the Southern way of life had nurtured from early colonial times. In New England geography and Puritanism fostered compact communities, interdependence and public discussion. In the South, climate and soil and an abundance of arable land promoted ruralism, and ruralism encouraged self-reliance and impeded the exchange of ideas. The introduction of slavery led to the establishment of the plantation system, and while planters were always a decided minority their prestige was such that they determined the pattern of behavior and set the tone of society. By law and by custom each planter became a petty sovereign. The chivalric code to which he subscribed made him hypersensitive to honor.

The domineering, individualistic quality which permeated Southern life was noted by many travellers who visited the land of Dixie in antebellum times. Alexis de Toqueville, for example, in his *Democracy in America,* observed that: "The citizen of the Southern states becomes a sort of domestic dictator from infancy; the first notion he acquires in life is that he was born to command, and the first habit he contracts is that of ruling without resistance. His education tends, then, to give him the character of a haughty and hasty man—irascible, violent, ardent in his desires, impatient of obstacles."

De Tocqueville, like Buckingham and Fanny Kemble, attributed much of the Southern imperiousness to slavery. This observation by visitors was shared by some of the natives. In 1787, George Mason stated in the Federal convention that slaves produced "a most pernicious effect on manners" and that every master was "a born petty tyrant." In 1860, a non-slaveholding woman said to a sister who had married a plantation owner: "You slaveholders have lived so long on your plantations with no one to gainsay or contradict you, and the negroes only looking up to you and worshiping you, that you expect to govern everybody and have it all your own way."

Whatever its origins and foundations, there can be no doubt that individualism was always strong in the South; by the time the Confederacy was established it had reached such a point among the upper classes that almost every man seemed inclined to think himself more capable of directing public affairs than those charged with that responsibility. Certainly the concept of full cooperation, of following the leader, of functioning as a member of the team, was very, very weak. On February 5, 1861, while the Confederate government was in process of organization, James H. Hammond wrote his good friend William

Gilmore Simms: *"Big-man-me-ism* reigns supreme & every one thinks every other a jealous fool or an aspiring knave." The characteristic which he dubbed so expressively was destined to increase. One who reads the writings of the period sometimes gets the impression that the aristocratic Southerner who staunchly supported the Davis government after the first year of war was a rarity. "Died of Big-man-me-ism" would not be an inappropriate epitaph for the Southern Confederacy.

A second possible reason for excessive contentiousness among Confederates was habit, developed during the long and bitter controversy with the North over slavery and states rights. Southerners participated in this controversy with greater feeling and in relatively greater numbers than Northerners because they were the minority and a dwindling one at that, because they regarded the threat to slavery as a direct menace to their way of life and because they had more leisure for brooding and recrimination than did Northerners. The slavery controversy was in a sense merely incidental to the life of Northerners who especially in the 1840's and 1850's were deeply absorbed in industrial development, westward expansion and the accumulation of wealth, while to Southerners this controversy was life itself. So, denunciation of the North became a major industry among Southerners in the decades before the war, and quarreling was deeply ingrained in their mode of life.

After secession removed the North as a principal source of contention, Southerners, from long addiction to controversy, turned on each other. To be sure there was a honeymoon of harmony, but before they had been under their own government a year, they were attacking

Jefferson Davis and other Confederate leaders as vehemently as they had ever denounced the Yankees.

A third cause of dissension among Confederates was frustration. A "nation with nothing" found that the waging of a great war with a country rich in all essential resources was a formidable undertaking. Improvisation and skimping were fun at first, and early successes on the battlefield inspired an assurance that inconveniences would be short-lived. But when self-sacrifice and devotion failed to bring quick victory, the public mood changed. New measures, calling for increased inconvenience and self-denial, were resorted to by the government, with hopeful statements as to consequences. What resulted was not a turn of the tide but greater disaster and increased deprivation. As months passed into years, and the South grew weaker while the North appeared stronger and more determined, an ever increasing number of Southerners realized the hopelessness of their cause. The prospect of defeat was exceedingly embittering. In their disillusionment and disappointment the people became more and more irritable and testy. They sought scapegoats for their unhappy and unexpected plight. In their frustration they lashed out at each other, and angry, unreasoning controversy became rife throughout the Confederacy.

Another possible cause of inordinate quarrelsomeness among Confederates was a sense of guilt about slavery. The Old South was orthodox, Calvinist and evangelical. Its people were acutely aware of sin and believed strongly that divine displeasure and punishment were normal consequences of wrong-doing.

It is a well-known fact that slavery was widely

regarded as an evil among Southerners of the late eighteenth and early nineteenth centuries. But the development of the cotton gin made the land of Dixie the land of cotton in the 1800's, and slavery became a profitable and seemingly indispensable form of labor, as well as a convenient mode of social control. In the 1830's, as slavery was becoming firmly fastened on the South, the Garrisonian abolitionists launched an aggressive attack on the institution; and, in the years that followed, Northern hostility to human bondage became more widespread. The combined effect of mounting opposition without and increasing material returns within was to suppress the egalitarian and humanitarian ideals of the Jeffersonian age and to cause Southerners to rationalize the rightness of slavery. At first they took the position that it was a necessary evil; they eventually declared it a positive good. Southern theologians played a leading role in proclaiming the righteous and ennobling influences of human bondage on master and slave alike.

But conviction of the wrongness of slavery smoldered in many Southern minds. In 1833, Mary Minor Blackford of Fredericksburg, Virginia, who later sent five sons to the Confederate army, wrote in her diary: "Disguise it as thou wilt, Slavery thou art a bitter draught. . . . I am convinced that the time will come when we shall look back and wonder how Christians could sanction slavery." This noble woman fought slavery as long as it existed and when emancipation finally came at the end of the war she exclaimed, "Praise be the Lord." She was able to remain in the South in spite of her known hostility to the institution, but she exercised considerable restraint in avowing her position. Most Southerners who openly denounced slavery were forced into exile.

Outward conformity did not necessarily mean inner acceptance, and uneasiness about slavery gnawed at numerous Southern consciences. These qualms were not allayed by secession and the setting up of a new government. Among prominent Confederates who deplored slavery were Robert E. Lee, Joseph E. Johnston, Matthew Fontaine Maury and A. P. Hill. In November, 1861, Mary Boykin Chesnut at the conclusion of a long apology that plainly revealed a troubled conscience wrote in her diary: "We are human beings of the nineteenth century, and slavery has to go of course . . . I hate slavery." A little earlier Eli Carruthers, Presbyterian minister of Alamance, North Carolina, who had regarded slavery as morally wrong for many years, was dismissed by his elders because he prayed that members of his congregation who were away in the Confederate army "might be . . . returned in safety though engaged in a bad cause."

When the tide of war turned against the South the guilt complex became more oppressive and some devoted Southerners who were honest with themselves confessed the conviction that God was punishing the South for its sin of slavery. On October 25, 1862, Herschel V. Johnson wrote Judge A. E. Cochran: "As to slavery, I think its days are numbered. The first gun at Sumter tolled its funereal dirge, I have a sort of undefined notion that God . . . is permitting us by our own folly to work out the emancipation of our slaves." About the same time a young Louisiana woman, registered satisfaction when one of her mother's slaves made good his escape, and after the conflict she wrote: "Always I felt the moral guilt of it, felt how impossible it must be for an owner of slaves to win his way to heaven."

As Confederate fortunes declined, a considerable number of Southerners became convinced that in clinging to slavery they were defying the moral sentiment of the world, and the consciousness of disapproval by Christian people everywhere made them extremely uncomfortable. In February, 1863, E. M. Bruce, Confederate Congressman from Kentucky, wrote to W. N. Haldeman: "The entire civilized world is hostile to the institution of slavery," and in December, 1864, Fred A. Porcher of South Carolina wrote Judah P. Benjamin: "Is it not manifest that it is this chasm [slavery] which has withheld from us the sympathy and cooperation of the great powers of Europe? Are we not fighting against the moral sense of the world? Can we hope to succeed in such a struggle?"

One remembers Queen Gertude's statement in *Hamlet:* "The lady protests too much methinks." No far-fetched psychology is required to inspire the idea that this spiritual turmoil about slavery, this sense of wrong-doing, this conviction that in keeping fellow human beings in bondage they were shocking the moral sensibilities of the civilized world, tended to make Southerners ill at ease with themselves and more touchy in their relations one with the other.

* * * * *

Closely related to the failure of harmony in the Confederacy was a second major shortcoming that was hardly less injurious. This was the failure of public information. The people did not know what was happening; why it was happening; or what their role in crucial events might be.

Neither state nor Confederate authorities had a program of news dissemination, and not until 1863 did the newspapers establish a press association. There were no presidential news releases; no public relations agencies; no systematic way of assembling and releasing official news.

From the beginning the government followed a policy of secrecy. The executive department guarded its activities from the public. Such a thing as a fireside chat from Jefferson Davis is wholly inconceivable. He was reluctant to reveal his doings even to Congress. Congress also was committed to the principle of secrecy from its earliest sessions. This close-mouthed policy was deeply resented by the press and by the people and it unquestionably was a serious mistake—one of the greatest in the whole realm of Confederate activity.

Neither Davis nor Congress ever seemed to realize the necessity of winning the hearts and minds of the people and of making them full partners in the struggle by keeping them amply and promptly informed about what was going on. The costliness of their failure was strikingly attested by an Alabama private who in March, 1862, wrote to a friend: "Trying to fight for something and I don't no what they ar quarling about myself, and I dont think any body els knows what they are fighting about."

A few, but unfortunately all too few, Confederate leaders realized the error of the government's secretive policy, and protested against it. In June, 1861, Mallory urged Davis to explain through the newspapers the circumstances which necessitated the abandonment of Harper's Ferry. The following summer Herschel V. Johnson wrote Alexander Stephens: "I hope Congress will now drop the practice of Secret Sessions except on very special occasions." In August, 1863, Senator James Phelan of Mississippi wrote Davis: "I do assure you the public sentiment of this state is in a most deplorable condition. . . . I wish you could meet the people . . . in mass meeting at a few points. It would effect a vast deal of good at this crisis." But the most pointed commentary on the subject was that of Congressman Henry C. Chambers of Mississippi who told his colleagues in the House on November 10, 1864: "We who sit here and who might have more fully advised them [the people] of the relations of all important questions to events as they arose, and so have assisted in forming and preserving a healthy tone of public sentiment, have perhaps too often sealed our lips or closed our doors—until the people, ceasing to look to us for instruction or sympathy, at last manifested no doubtful indications of finding conclusions without our assistance. . . . The public mind is at present confused, perplexed, troubled. . . . Let us throw off the shackles of over-caution as to criticism of men and measures and freely confessing abuses, charge home the responsibility for their existence, and invite both Government and people to hear. It is a great mistake to suppose our people cannot bear the whole truth on every and any question . . . and from our enemies there is no longer anything to be concealed."

As previously noted, Davis made some appearances among the people to tell them of major events and policies, but two of his public relations tours were made after Gettysburg and Vicksburg, and hence came too late to be of much good. And he never visited the Trans-

Mississippi Department, where his presence was most needed.

The necessity of an effective program of public information was all the more urgent and the lack of such a program all the more damaging, in view of the nature of the Confederate cause, the unusual character of some of its policies and the background of its people. In seceding and setting up a separate government, nine million Southerners (including three and a half million Negroes most of whom probably hoped for Confederate defeat), were defying twenty-two million Northerners, who had a well established government and an enormous advantage in material resources. Assuming that Northerners, would fight to preserve the Union (and Davis thought they would) the South's only hope of establishing its independence lay in bringing the full weight of its limited strength to bear on the North; and the more quickly it could do so, the greater the likelihood of success. A full and quick employment of its strength meant that the control of its resources must be centralized. But centralization ran counter to the concept of local rights which was deeply imbedded in tradition and written into the Constitution. The mobilization of public sentiment would have been important under any circumstances; in view of the fact that the people were to be called on to accept a concentration of authority that violated their basic philosophy, it became absolutely imperative.

Yet, virtually no effort was made by Confederate leaders to prepare the minds of the people for the revolutionary changes that secession and war entailed. The extreme disunionists in their initial eagerness rushed secession through to adoption without allowing full opportunity for public discussion and in most instances without referring the secession ordinances to popular vote. It is not meant to imply that secession would have been rejected, for the majority undoubtedly favored separation at the time the ordinances were adopted. But the minority would have gone along in much better spirit if they had been allowed to have their say, and the effects of a referendum would have had beneficial results on the people as a whole. The fire-eating element employed the same headlong and high-handed procedures in setting up the Confederate government. The constitution was drawn up in great haste and was not referred to the people. The same body that drew up the constitution, a body chosen by state conventions and not by popular ballot, assumed legislative functions and for a year acted as the national law-making assembly without obtaining public sanction. Moderates, most of whom were of Whig background, deeply resented the steamroller tactics of the fire-eaters, who usually were Democrats. Especially did the moderates resent the tendency of "ultras" to brand them as traitors because of their failure in the beginning to climb on the secession bandwagon.

With the "ultras" in control, riding high on the initial thrust of patriotism, the government squelched or ignored opposition and took not the time nor the trouble to show the masses that state sovereignty would have to be temporarily restricted while the nation waged an all-out war in which that principle was a basic issue. The dominant group and its methods met little opposition as long as all went well on the battlefield and prospects of a quick victory were good. But when the tide of conflict turned and the delusion of an easy triumph faded, a reaction set in, many of the fire-eaters were thrown out of office and the government had hard going throughout the remainder of the conflict. Emotion may suffice for launching a conflict, but Confederate experience indicates its insufficiency to support the conduct of a war, and especially a long, hard one.

Certainly Confederate leaders blundered in not preparing the minds of their people for such unprecedented, drastic and onerous measures as conscription, heavy taxation, impressment, crop control, suspension of habeas corpus and the arming of slaves. Even with careful and extensive preparation these measures would have aroused considerable opposition. But to spring them on an uninformed citizenry not accustomed to strong governmental controls meant that they were doomed to almost certain failure.

Another area in which public information was notoriously weak was that of military events. The minds of the people were not prepared for crippling military reverses such as Roanoke Island, Fort Donelson, New Orleans and Vicksburg. Hence, these disasters struck with tremendous impact and sent an enormous shock throughout the land. The effects were worsened by the inability of the people to get accurate reports of events promptly after they occurred. Newspapers continued to inform their readers of great victories for days and even weeks after such enormous catastrophes as Vicksburg and Gettysburg.

On July 25, 1863, Thomas H. Duval of Austin, Texas, wrote in his diary: "Went into town—Got extra and found it confirmed all about the taking of Washington, Harrisburg, etc. Also that Grant had attacked

Johnston at Jackson and been utterly defeated. . . . The news glorious for our side."

The diary of Kate Stone, who was residing in Lamar County, Texas, in 1863, reveals that she thought the Confederates victorious at Vicksburg until late July and that in early August she was still under the impression that Lee had captured Washington and Philadelphia. On August 10, 1863, she noted: "Our list of victories last month were all a mistake. Gen. Lee has recrossed into Virginia. . . . We do not hold, nor have we destroyed a single Northern city as we so much hoped. A dark hour for the Confederacy. The loss of Vicksburg has stunned the whole country."

Misinformation of the sort revealed by these two diarists lessened the confidence of the people in the press and the government. Many Southerners must have felt as J. H. Hammond who wrote on April 16, 1864, to William Gilmore Simms: "I wish they would fight a real battle somewhere & tell us the truth about it."

On January 5, 1864, a Texan wrote Governor Pendleton Murrah: "Our recent reverses in Tenn. are not understood. . . . All ungraciously acknowledge a defeat. No disposition is manifested to converse about it. The people are mortified and they have a right to be, when every telegram, report, and news letter assured them that 'Bragg was master of the situation.' It is cruel to deceive the people with a hope they were so fain to cherish. The burthens of the war is beginning to tell on the patriotism of the people."

One of the most striking evidences of the failure of public information was in respect to Jefferson Davis. The Confederate President was not sold to the people. He did not reveal himself to his constituents and he was misrepresented by the press and the leaders. After the first year of the war, especially, he was pictured as a power-hungry politician bent on establishing a dictatorship. Davis's shortcomings, as previously stated, were numerous and grievous but a hankering for dictatorship was not among them. Far from being a despot, he exercised with notable restraint the enormous power conferred upon him. But because he was misunderstood his leadership was impaired.

Owing to misinformation and lack of understanding concerning leaders, policies and events, rumor ran riot in the Confederacy and people came to view with suspicion and distrust those persons and agencies who should have done most to sustain their spirits. Private Charles Anthony probably reflected a widespread sentiment when he wrote on January 19, 1865: "Editors and Newspaper scribbes have been the cause of 'much of our present gloom—by holding out bright ideas under false colors. I believe it is best to let the truth always be knew, even if it is disagreeable."

The failure of public information in the Confederacy was due in part, of course, to inadequate transportation and communication. As George Edgar Turner has so effectively pointed out in *Victory Rode the Rails,* the North's well-developed rail and water network helped promote on the Union side a degree of cohesiveness not attainable in the South; and this, along with a tremendous edge in journalistic facilities, gave Northerners an enormous advantage in disseminating information and sustaining morale. Even so, the South could have made a better use of what it had.

* * * * *

A third important failure of the Confederacy was the failure of flexibility. Throughout the antebellum period the South had remained predominantly agricultural, rural and provincial, while the North was becoming industrial, urban and national. Millions of foreigners poured into the North in the decades immediately preceding the Civil War, bringing new ideas, new skills and new ways. The flood of immigration, the expansion of industry, the growth of cities and the increase of wealth gave Northern life zestfulness and elasticity, afforded valuable experience in large-scale enterprise and brought to the people an enlarged vision of the nation's greatness and power.

Southern life, on the other hand, relatively uninfluenced by immigration, hemmed in by an intellectual blockade for the protection of slavery and enchained by an agricultural economy, tended to be static, conservative and sectional. To put it another way, Southerners drew back in a shell, assumed a defensive posture, planted cotton, proclaimed the blessings of slavery, denounced Yankees and "furriners" and hoarded the treasures of the past, while the North and other parts of the world, responding to the blandishments of "progress," marched off and left them.

When, in the spring of 1861, the South found itself involved in war, it was a new kind of war: one in which railroads, steamships, massive armies and vast distances played an important role. It was a war which had to be sustained by factories, skilled laborers and trained managers. It called for large-scale activity, close coordination and expert administration. It was modern war. It was big business. Its successful prosecution required varied talents, ready adaptation and the ability to think big thoughts.

Notwithstanding remarkable achievement in many areas of endeavor, the fact remains that the agrarian and provincial South, bound by its old ways and concepts, was not sufficiently flexible to wage a modern war against the modern nation that its adversary had become.

The South's political leaders did not break away from the localism to which they were tied by custom and preference. State governors in varying degree insisted on organizing troops, appointing officers, hoarding supplies, controlling transportation and influencing military operations within their respective boundaries. Davis was so thoroughly imbued with the doctrine of local rights that he sometimes failed to exercise the central authority conferred upon him by Congress. In April, 1863, the Confederate lawmakers passed an act giving the President virtually supreme control over railroads, but Davis never took anything like full advantage of this important measure. Robert C. Black in his excellent book, *Railroads of the Confederacy,* declares that the President "appeared smitten by a fatal hesitation." "Nearly every carrier represented a state, county or municipal interest," he adds, and "Jefferson Davis found himself enmeshed in the strands of his own [state rights] philosophy."

Provincialism was of course not peculiar to the leaders of the Confederacy. The hold which it had on the people generally is well illustrated by the statement of an upcountry South Carolinian to John W. DeForest after the war: "I'll give you my notion of things," said the

Southerner; "I go first for Greenville, then for Greenville District, then for the up-country, then for South Carolina, then for the South, then for the United States; and after that I don't go for anything. I've no use for Englishmen, Turks and Chinese."

In a large measure, owing to widespread addiction to state rights, the Confederacy tried to operate on the basis of eleven separate conflicts instead of merging its resources into one great centrally-directed war.

The setting up of a separate government and the conduct of a great modern war required a proficiency in large-scale administration. The Southern planters, lawyers, bankers and business men who had directed public and private affairs with reasonable success under the old union in times of peace were unable to cope with the new and larger responsibilities thrust upon them by secession and conflict. The capacity for organizing and managing extensive and complex activities was sadly lacking in the Confederacy.

Want of administrative ability was notoriously prevalent among government officials. It was also a salient weakness among generals. The South produced an impressive number of brilliant combat commanders but it had no full general who was outstanding both in battle and in administration. Lee came nearest to achieving distinction in both capacities. But he failed to develop an efficient staff, his orders were sometimes lacking in clarity, and some of his campaigns were poorly coordinated.

The Confederacy's command and staff systems, as Professor T. Harry Williams and others have pointed out, were considerably inferior to those of the North. The South had eight full generals, while the North's top brass consisted of one lieutenant general. But when it came to staff, the group that actually administers an army and coordinates its activities, the Confederacy was shockingly stingy. Lee's staff was headed by a colonel, while that of the Army of the Potomac had several brigadiers and the chief of staff was a major general. The North adopted a unified command in March, 1864, with Lincoln at the top, Grant as general-in-chief and Halleck in between as chief of staff. The Confederacy did not get around to unifying the control of its armies under a general-in-chief until February, 1865, when its cause was doomed.

The direction of Confederate military affairs suffered greatly from looseness and inefficiency throughout the war. In February, 1862, a regimental commander wrote Senator C. C. Clay from Tuscumbia, Alabama: "This valley seems entirely overlooked; [Albert Sidney] Johnston thinks it is in Beauregard's Department; Polk thinks it is in his; but nobody seems alive to its vast importance and few know even where it is." A similar lack of understanding and looseness of management was apparent in the conduct of the Vicksburg campaign. And confusion as to channels of communication and areas of jurisdiction as between Lee, Beauregard, Davis and Bragg greatly impaired operations around Richmond and Petersburg in May and June, 1864. During his incumbency as commander of the Trans-Mississippi Department, Kirby Smith was often troubled by uncertainty as to the extent of his authority.

The inflexibility underlying the looseness and mismanagement that characterized the South's conduct of the war was sharply and vividly expressed by L. M. Keitt, a

South Carolina general and ex-Confederate Congressman, in a series of letters written to his wife early in 1864. On January 22, he wrote: "[I] fear that our people have not risen to the height of this present crisis. . . . They have cherished state pride and exclusiveness for eighty years, and no changes however great, no ruin however appalling, could make them forget it for a moment. Our people will not move out of the old forms and routine."

Two days later he stated: "I wish with us that Genius and the hour were wedded. A planting people are always the victim of routine . . . in war a fatal defect."

On January 31, he observed: "You cannot have liaison, connection, unity among a planting community. . . . We are in mortal peril from our inability to govern ourselves." On February 11, he added: "Countries like ours are not fit for revolution. . . . Is it because there is no genius? No the land is full of it. . . . What is the cause of this? Our political institutions. In peace they make us great through our individuality; in war they make us weak through want of harmony and complete obedience to routine."

If by routine he meant, as he apparently did, slavish devotion to tradition, to an outlook that was limited, to an economy that was agrarian, to ways that were outmoded, he was hitting very close to the truth.

* * * * *

A fourth failure that helped lead the South down the road to Appomattox was the failure of judgement. This failure can be associated with its isolation and defense complex.

Shut off from the outside world and misled by wishful thinking, the South developed exaggerated ideas about its own strength. The thought, as stated in Confederate arithmetics, that one Southerner could whip at least seven Yankees was a silly one, but it did not seem so to the "brave Southrons" who bandied it about one hundred years ago. The people of Dixie in those days had talked so long and so loud of the superiority of themselves and their way of life that they had become victims of their own propaganda.

Southerners erred in their judgment of Europe. Most of them were thoroughly convinced that England, France and other nations were so completely dependent on cotton that they would quickly intervene, if necessary, to maintain the flow of fibre to their mills. They failed to take into account the huge surpluses of cotton and cloth that had accumulated in European warehouses in the period immediately preceding the war. They did not anticipate the resort by the outside world to expedients and substitutes to offset the cotton shortage. They did not foresee the counterbalancing effects of tremendous profits from the manufacture, shipping and sale to both belligerents of munitions and other commodities essential to war. Finally, they were blinded to the great hostility to slavery among those who would suffer most from the cotton famine, the working classes of the great textile centers. Southerners traveled extensively in Europe in the antebellum period, and they should have sensed that cotton was not king, but they were so habituated to accepting the pleasant and ignoring the unpleasant that they were impervious to the truth.

Southerners also misjudged their foes. They underestimated the North's industrial might and the mood and strength of its teeming population. They thought that

Northerners were so cowardly and so deeply concerned with material gain that they would not go to war; and that if they did, a battle or two would convert them to peace. Unaware of the tremendous influence of the rail and water lines that reached out from the East, they firmly believed that the West would not join in the conflict except as an ally of the South. They knew that antislavery sentiment was strong in the North, but they thought it was limited largely to the abolitionist wing of the Republican party. They were grossly ignorant of the enormous hold that this sentiment had on some of the immigrant groups and the strength that it had attained among Democrats.

The most serious error of Southerners in judging their foes was their failure to appreciate the depth of the North's devotion to the Union. In the period from 1820 to 1860 the North's political philosophy had undergone a transformation. The local and sectional outlook that lay back of the Hartford Convention had gradually given way to a strong national consciousness. Many influences had contributed to this evolution, among which were the strong nationalistic concepts of some of the immigrant groups and especially the Germans; an increasing realization of the benefits of a strong central government to industry and business; and the growing conviction that America, committed to the principle of freedom and democracy, was destined to be an example and a refuge for liberty-loving people everywhere. Southerners, not sharing the experiences which led to the North's conversion to the ideal of Union, had little awareness of the revolution that was taking place beyond the Mason and Dixon line. Because of ignorance the Southerner made the mistake first of thinking that the North would not risk a war to prevent the disruption of the Union and second, that it would not make a sustained and costly effort to restore it. Hence, Southern leaders with few exceptions proclaimed independence with light-heartedness and confidence, and after the first great victories looked hopefully to the North for signs of acceptance of separation. Had they realized that thousands upon thousands of young men from Wisconsin, Minnesota, Pennsylvania and Massachusetts and the other Northern states were willing to lay down their lives on the altar of Union, and that the folk at home would support them, these leaders probably would not have urged the people to secession, and if they had, they would have been constrained after the South's initial victories to gird them for a long and hard struggle.

But the Southern leaders and their people failed to comprehend the temper of the North and of Europe just as they failed to realize their own weaknesses. And these failures along with those of flexibility, public information, harmony, morale and leadership, were salient influences leading the South down the long and torturing way to Appomattox.

Study of these influences and their bearing on the course of the conflict indicates that the turning point in the struggle probably came in the spring of 1862 rather than in July, 1863, the usually accepted time. When the combined effects of Fort Henry, Fort Donelson and other military reverses are considered, along with the loss of confidence in leadership, the tremendous decline of public morale, the break between Davis and Congress, the enactment of laws deeply obnoxious to the people such as those providing for conscription and the suspension of habeas corpus—all of which date back to the early months of 1862—it becomes apparent that the South's ability to wage war effectively was severely and permanently curtailed. Its only hope of triumph after the spring of 1862, lay in the collapse of the North's determination to persevere in the struggle. When cognizance is taken of the strength among Northerners of the ideal of Union, the likelihood of such a collapse appears remote indeed. Even if Lee had won at Gettysburg and captured Washington, New York and Philadelphia, it seems extremely doubtful, in view of the North's devotion to the Union, that the outcome of the war would have been other than what it was.